An OPUS book

The Way People Work

THE ORIGINAL CAKERIE LTD.

Christine Howarth

The Way People Work

Job satisfaction and
the challenge of change

Oxford   New York

OXFORD UNIVERSITY PRESS

1984

Oxford University Press, Walton Street, Oxford OX2 6DP

London Glasgow New York Toronto
Delhi Bombay Calcutta Madras Karachi
Kuala Lumpur Singapore Hong Kong Tokyo
Nairobi Dar es Salaam Cape Town
Melbourne Auckland

and associated companies in
Beirut Berlin Ibadan Mexico City Nicosia

Oxford is a trade mark of Oxford University Press

First published 1984 as an Oxford University Press paperback
and simultaneously in a hardback edition

British Library Cataloguing in Publication Data
Howarth, Christine
The way people work - (An OPUS book)
1. Job satisfaction
I. Title
658.3'1422   HF5549.5.J63
ISBN 0-19-219168-3
ISBN 0-19-289155-3 Pbk

Library of Congress Cataloging in Publication Data
Howarth, Christine.
The way people work. (OPUS)
Bibliography: p.   Includes index.
1. Job satisfaction.   2. Personnel management
3. Psychology, Industrial.   I. Title.   II. Series.
HF5549.5.J63H66   1984   658.3'1422   83-17287
ISBN 0-19-219168-3
ISBN 0-19-289155-3 (pbk.)

Set by Colset Private Ltd.
Printed in Great Britain by
Richard Clay (The Chaucer Press) Ltd.
Bungay, Suffolk

Preface

Throughout the industrialized world there are organizations in trouble: they are not doing efficiently the jobs they set out to do. Manufacturing organizations are finding their ability to produce hampered by industrial relations difficulties caused, on the face of it, by trivia. Service organizations in both private and public sectors are frequently so bogged down in their own internal systems that their staff are unable to respond properly to the needs of their customers. The result is that a good deal of potential is not being realized. People are suffering: as customers, as shareholders and as employees.

Over the last fifteen years or so I have been working with a number of organizations who are trying to do something about this problem. This book is about how the people working in these organizations feel: how they feel about their jobs; how they are managed; and how their organizations serve their customers. It is about how their feelings affect the performance of their organizations. And it is about how some of the problems created can be alleviated.

Like a doctor the outside adviser tends to see those with difficulties. But this book is not just for those who feel they have some kind of problem. Many organizations who would consider themselves basically healthy are not, in fact, performing at their peak, and may even be allowing early signs of trouble to go unrecognized. By attending to these symptoms they may be able to build upon their strengths and improve their performance still further. As one personnel director put it, 'I don't think there is much wrong with my company. But why be content with a horse that can jump a five foot fence when with the right kind of extra effort you can get it to jump a seven foot fence?'

I have written this book for managers, trade unionists and advisers – indeed for anyone concerned with helping organizations to work better, in the interests both of their customers and of the people who work in them. No panacea is offered: just information about what people in similar positions have tried to do; in what ways they have succeeded and why; in what ways they have failed and why; and how they felt about it.

It is a book written from the practical point of view of a consultant whose job it is to give people the confidence and insight to come to grips with their problems and to improve their ability to use their experience and ideas in solving them. Not all consultants see their job this way. Some are too strongly attached to their role as the 'expert' who does things for, or to, people to wish to help them to do these things for themselves. Others, who identify a fundamental conflict of interest between 'workers' and 'employers', feel that my way of working encourages what one of their school has called 'a politically unacceptable identity of interest between workers and employers'. I readily accept that conflicts of interest exist at work, and that probably they always will. But I do not accept that they should necessarily stand in the way of people trying to improve the way they spend their lives.

I hope my approach and the case studies that I describe will help people to take a fresh look at what is happening to them, to build upon their strong points, to tackle their difficulties more successfully, and to improve the quality of their working lives and of the services they offer to their customers.

The book is divided into three parts. Part I, 'Working in organizations', looks at the problem facing many organizations today: that of managing to thrive in the unpredictable modern world. It sets out some of the main signs of danger; the major social and economic factors behind the problem; some of the theories which help to explain people's behaviour in these circumstances; and how attempts to help organizations to improve the way they work have developed over recent years.

Part II, 'Organizations at work', describes what some prominent organizations have done to cope with this problem in practice. It does so through three case studies taken from the motor manufacturing industry, the Italian metal working industry, and the British Civil Service.

Part III, 'Working better', concludes the book with a review of some practical ideas for helping people and their organization to work better.

I should make it clear that throughout the book views expressed about the Civil Service and the work of its Job Satisfaction Team are my own, based on ten years' expercence of working with them as an outside adviser.

Contents

Acknowledgements

Many people have helped me to complete this book and to all of them my thanks are due. In particular I acknowledge the professional advice and friendly support of the Work Research Unit, especially of Oliver Tynan, its Director. (I hope he will not find too much with which to disagree.)

I would also like to thank my family and friends, who put up with me while I was working on it. I should mention especially Verona Howarth, my mother-in-law, (I hope she now understands what I do when I disappear for the day) and my husband, Duncan, who tried to teach me to write.

London   C. H.
May 1983

PART I

Working in organizations

1 Where things go wrong

This book is about coping with a problem which to a greater or lesser extent bothers all kinds of organizations in both private and public sectors: that of keeping in step with the rapidly changing world in which they must operate.

The fundamental social, economic, political and technological changes taking place today inevitably affect the attitudes of the two main groups of people with whom an organization must deal: its customers and its employees. Nowadays both are more demanding. The 'professional customer' of today wants a high standard of individual service as well as good quality products and competitive prices; today's employees expect not only to earn a decent living, but also to get some personal satisfaction out of doing so. They are concerned about the quality of their working experience, just as customers are concerned about the quality of the service they receive. Both groups wish to be treated as people rather than as 'the consumer' or 'the workforce'.

This book focuses primarily (though not entirely) on what organizations can do to respond more fully to their employees' changing needs. This is not because I think the customer is less important, but because I feel that only by making the most of the skills, experience and initiative of their employees can organizations stand a chance of responding to their customers' higher expectations, or indeed to any of the social, economic, political and technological changes that lie ahead.

Because it is the only secure basis for any enterprise, it makes good business sense for organizations to ask if they are allowing their employees to contribute enough and to find ways of encouraging and enabling them to contribute more. It is not only a moral argument; it is a practical one.

The underlying problem is that many organizations are out of step with the changing expectations of their employees. Although the consequences of this problem can be serious, its presence is not always suspected partly because it tends to show indirectly in different symptoms which vary in effect from threatening to bring the whole enterprise to a standstill to creating a vague feeling that things are not going as well as they might be. Whatever the degree of seriousness of these symptoms it is worth examining them because they show that the organization is needlessly wasting its resources and performing below its potential.

These symptoms, or danger signs, are often more apparent to an outsider than to a manager or trade union representative within. They are to be discerned in what people at all levels feel about the work that they do; how they are managed; and how their organization serves its customers. People often talk about such feelings only to an outsider, partly because there is not normally any opportunity or requirement to make them known on the job; partly because they do not think that anyone from within really wants to know how they feel; and partly because it often takes an outside stimulus to get people to recognize and articulate feelings which the organization has hitherto ignored.

For the same kinds of reasons, the outsider also notices the positive side: the strong points on which an organization can build, the ideas that people have for increasing their own contribution and for improving the way their organization operates.

Because understanding the problem must be the first step towards putting things right, let us look first at the danger signs. They are the key to what might be wrong. If people have any of the following feelings about the work they do the organization has a problem:

(i)   it bores them,
(ii) it offers little challenge,
(iii) it carries less responsibility than they would like,
(iv) it gives them no sense of achievement,
(v)   it allows little scope for them to develop their skills,
(vi) it offers only limited chances of advancement.

These symptoms are all to do with the job itself. There are other danger signs. It is not just their work that determines how people feel. They are also affected by the way they are managed. For instance, a person may find his work potentially very satisfying – the problem may be that his boss is always breathing down his neck and preventing him from getting on with it, or that he is required to consult headquarters every time a decision has to be made.

So an organization has a problem if its employees have any of the following feelings about the way their work is managed:

(i)   it gives them too little discretion in key decisions,
(ii) it allows them too little control over matters that affect them,
(iii) it stops them getting feedback about how they are doing.

But why are these danger signs? The answer is simply that people do not work well if they have such feelings about their jobs. The great majority of people want to do their jobs well. If their jobs interest them, give them scope to use and develop their abilities and experience, to meet challenges, take responsibility and to advance their careers then they will try to do them well. Their talents will be fully used. They will get satisfaction and their organization's customers will benefit. If jobs are not of this kind, people's abilities will be wasted and people will not try to do their jobs particularly well. They will not find satisfaction and neither will their customers, inside or outside the organization.

This is true of people at all levels and in all functions. In the words of some of Saab's American advertisements: 'Bored people build bad cars'. They also make unhelpful shop assistants and unresponsive officials of local and central government.

It is perhaps less obvious the further up the hierarchy one looks. But the manager who feels over-constrained is very likely to over-constrain his subordinates, just as the specialist who feels his expertise is undervalued is unlikely to care much about the quality of the advice he gives.

This may seem fairly simple and straightforward. Why then is the problem not more generally identified and tackled? There are all kinds of reasons for this – economic, legal, financial and technological. But perhaps the main reason is that people, in real life, do not tell their boss that they could do their job better if it offered them more scope. They themselves are probably not aware that this is the case, but, even if they were, they would not expect their boss to show much concern. Instead, their frustration shows indirectly in ways which may appear to say more about them as employees than about the organization and its jobs.

The most common manifestations of this underlying frustration are defiance, seemingly irrational pay claims, and apathy. Outright defiance is the most obvious of these and strikes and other forms of industrial action are the most extreme examples. The test is not to see that there is a problem, but rather to recognize what the problem is. Defiance tends to unsettle those who have to deal with it. They interpret it as a personal attack. In self-defence they blame the disruption on those who have apparently caused it. They do not look beyond the 'bloody-mindedness' of the workers and their trade union representatives.

But concealed behind this apparent bloody-mindedness can be useful information. Of course there are people who really are aiming at disruption, but there are far more who are just protesting about the frustrations of their jobs in the only way they feel is open. Another reason may be that the trade unionists who represent frustrated people have themselves taken the office because it gives them an outlet for talents which they feel are wasted in their normal work. Representing others is something in which pride can be taken. It can be varied and interesting, offering great scope for initiative. It can bring status, recognition and power and it is often far more challenging and rewarding than the normal jobs of the representatives. Where these normal jobs are really frustrating, becoming a trade union representative can seem the only chance to get back at an organization which wastes the employees' talents and fails to seek their views.

The result can be hard-fought disputes in which both sides have more at stake than is apparent on the surface. Such disputes often centre on what looks like a demand for more pay. These have become increasingly common and increasingly hard fought. The problems seem to be obvious. People are asking for more money and, very likely, they genuinely want more money, especially when both prices and expectations are rising. But if they do not find their jobs rewarding they may be asking for more than money: for intangible benefits like self-respect and self-fulfilment, if not at work, then outside.

Their real demand may be an unconscious one that cannot be articulated. But even if it were articulated, it might not be understood by organizations who do not suspect that such needs exist. The conclusion the organization tends to reach is that these people are greedy. But this conclusion, understandable though it may be, does not help because it evades the real problem which must be solved.

Defiance and disputes are overt expressions of frustration. Less overt, but far more widespread is apathy. This may take many forms. People may be late or absent from work for trivial reasons. They may be mildly obstructive – not necessarily openly hostile, but just not as co-operative as they might be. They may leave customers waiting while they chat on the phone, finish filling in a form, or fiddle with the way their merchandise is displayed. In the factory they may just stand by and watch the faulty production go on down the line where quality control is expected to pick it out.

This kind of indifference may show up in quality control or personnel statistics, but it is often too subtle a matter to be measured. This is increasingly so the higher up the organization one looks, and it is often most difficult to detect, most difficult to treat and most damaging in its effects amongst managers. How a manager feels about his job affects not only the way he does his own job, but also how his subordinates do theirs and how they feel about it. A manager who does not care is likely to have staff who do not care.

But why do such people apparently not care? On the surface it may look as if they are just that kind of person: not terribly interested in a career; not personally inclined to take responsibility or make a conscientious effort; or just bone idle. Of course there are people like this. But there are many more who come to behave like this because they are out of sympathy with the nature of their work and the way in which it is organized and managed.

An organization which stresses central control at the expense of local autonomy may feel it is reducing the risk of people making uninformed, embarrassing and costly decisions. This may be so in part. But it may also prevent them from using their local knowledge and experience for the benefit of the organization and its customers. An organization which emphasizes the need to adhere to internal procedures rather than the need to do the job in the best possible way may achieve uniformity of procedure. But in achieving this it may silence constructive criticism; dull initiative and enthusiasm; and leave its customers feeling that they have been treated like numbers rather than people.

The trouble is that when people behave as if they were indifferent they reinforce their organization's assumption that employees these days are inclined to be slipshod unless they are told exactly what to do and then checked to ensure that they have done it. The resulting emphasis on uniformity and centrally imposed control can thus aggravate the very problem that the organization needs to solve.

Organizations have a feel about them. Healthy, successful organizations feel positive and confident. They face facts and try to adapt to circumstances. They make the most of the people they employ. They give staff at all levels scope to use their abilities and their initiative. The job of their managers is to bring out the best in people. Such organizations want to know about their strengths and weaknesses and so encourage, listen to and act on constructive criticism whether from employees, trade unionists, outside advisers, customers or even shareholders.

The people that work in such organizations tend to be positive and confident too. They say what they think. They welcome responsibility and take a pride in trying to improve their performance. They have a clear idea of a 'customer', whether inside or outside the organization, and get their satisfaction from doing a good job for that customer. If their organization is unionized they tend to play an active part in trade union affairs, making sure their union represents their views accurately and constructively.

Organizations in trouble are not like this. They feel anxious. They do not face facts. Lacking the confidence to change, they deny that adaptation is necessary. They wish their employees were of a higher calibre, that their trade unionists were less disruptive and their customers less difficult to please. Because they do not feel their staff are trustworthy and competent they prescribe their tasks in detail and limit their responsibilities. They use their managers to ensure compliance and back this up with central control. They do not want to know what people think unless this reinforces the status quo.

The people that work in such organizations may occasionally be disruptive, but they are more likely to be passive. They do not say what they think because they are not accustomed to anyone wanting to know. Often they do not think very much about their work at all because there is little point. They probably do as they are told, but they do not take much pride in their work because it does not enable them to feel pride. The 'customer' has far less reality to them than the internal procedures that must be followed. If their organization is unionized they tend to be apathetic about trade union affairs, leaving others to represent their views whether accurately and constructively or not.

What is needed is a change of spirit so that organizations with problems like these acquire the confidence to tackle them – but not in the expectation that they can be neatly solved and all conflicts of interest settled. Many of the tensions which cause such difficulties within an organization actually originate outside it and are, in many ways, beyond its control. And the difficulties which do originate inside are likely to be deeply rooted in past experience which cannot easily be set aside.

Even as people try to clarify the nature of their difficulties, the situation goes on evolving and new problems and conflicts of interest are encountered. Being realistic about this is the mainspring of the confidence which enables people to adapt to what is going on around them. The first step towards this realism is to seek to understand the obvious symptoms; to see beyond the apparent defiance, greed or indifference of their employees, the 'bloody-mindedness' of their trade union representatives and the niggles of their customers to what is really going on and why.

2 Why things go wrong

One of the difficulties in helping organizations to understand such problems as these is that they are by no means new. Because such problems are not new there is a tendency to assume that they do not matter. It is as if it were quite acceptable, indeed inevitable, that organizations should struggle on, performing at less than their peak, simply because they have become accustomed to doing so.

But the major difficulty is that such problems are ultimately the result of failing to adapt to wide-ranging economic and social changes which are themselves extremely complex and hard to fathom – particularly when we are all involved in them and affected by them. This kind of change is beyond the control of an individual or an organization. Our reaction is often to let such changes happen and somehow to try to live with the consequences, rather than to analyse what is going on and make conscious efforts to adapt.

Some managers and trade unionists feel such changes should simply be stopped or, better still, reversed. Then the problems would go away. As one manager said to a group of his colleagues who were discussing how such changes affected them as managers: 'social change is not a good thing. We must stop it'. Most people would not express their attitude so categorically, but still many of us prefer to wish intractable problems away rather than face up to them. It is crucially important that key managers and trade unionists in an organization come to terms with the inevitability of economic and social change and learn to regard it not as something which must either overwhelm or be resisted, but rather as a challenge to which it is possible to react positively.

However, let us look first not at these changes, but at people's behaviour. It is important, now more than ever before, for managers and trade unionists to understand why people behave as they do because it is this behaviour that brings social change home to organizations and makes it necessary for them to adapt.

The psychology of people at work

When managers and trade unionists puzzle over their problems they are, in effect, seeking the answers to some fundamental questions like: what do people look for in their jobs nowadays? what are the effects of managing them in different ways? how do people feel about their jobs? what leads them to do their jobs well or badly? Put more simply, why do people behave as they do at work or, even more simply, why do people behave as they do? After all, each of us is the same person whether at work or outside.

There is more than fifty years' research in behavioural science which addresses itself to such questions, not all of it particularly pertinent or helpful. But by the 1960s certain common themes were beginning to emerge and these are now well accepted. While this is not a book about behavioural science theory, it is useful to outline some of the work by the researchers who, I have found, help people most: Abraham Maslow, Douglas McGregor and Frederick Herzberg. What did they have to say?

Maslow: What people need from their jobs [1]

Maslow was somewhat unusual amongst psychologists in that his theory was based upon the study of healthy, mature people whose approach to life is based on realism rather than fantasy. This in itself makes his views worth considering. Human behaviour, said Maslow, is influenced very largely, though not entirely, by our attempts to satisfy certain needs. These needs are arranged in a hierarchy of five levels, ranging from the 'basic' to the 'higher level'. The basic needs must always be satisfied before we can concentrate on anything else. The most basic need is for food and drink. People who never have enough to eat and drink are never able to concern themselves with much else. And if at any time we become hungry and thirsty our concentration on 'higher level' things is weakened until we have satisfied our hunger and thirst. This 'slip back', as some call it, is another feature of Maslow's theory.

When the need for food and drink is satisfied we become concerned with 'safety', the need for shelter and protection, for freedom from fear and pain, for a sense of order and predictability in our world. When we are well-nourished and reasonably secure we then, said Maslow, begin to feel the need for affection and friendship, the need to identify with a particular group.

None of this is very surprising. Most of us would accept these three needs as common and important. But Maslow went further. Well-fed people with reasonably secure lives, and warm relationships with family and friends, would now turn their attention to the 'higher level' needs. First they would become concerned with the need for 'esteem', both self-esteem and the deserved esteem of others. At the peak of the pyramid comes the need for what Maslow termed 'self-actualization' – the need to make the most of our own potential, whatever that may be, whether as artist, production worker, clerk, sportsman, home-decorator or parent.

What Maslow said, in effect, is that all of us share the higher level needs just as we share those that are more basic. We all need to earn respect and to feel that we are using and developing our abilities, just as we all need food and shelter. And, moreover, we need these things whether we are at home or at work. If our needs are not met, or are frustrated, whether at home or work, we suffer. Our physical health suffers if we are deprived of adequate nourishment. Just as surely, said Maslow, our mental health suffers if we are deprived of the opportunity to earn respect and to realize our potential. And mental deprivation has its consequences as does physical deprivation. Instead of behaving as healthy, positive, responsible adults we lose the sense of our own abilities and with it our confidence. We decide that many of the things we are capable of doing are just not worth the effort. Instead of our being in control of events, we become their victims. As employees we are at best compliant, but we may lack initiative, drive and even a sense of responsibility.

In Maslow's view therefore, an organization cannot operate anywhere near its optimum, nor base itself securely for the future, without giving its employees scope to satisfy their needs for personal development. A hard-headed, business-like approach to enduring profitability requires attention to what is often regarded as a 'soft' concern with employees as people.

The work of Maslow on human need has been enriched and amplified by other researchers, many of them using different starting points. One of these, Douglas McGregor, concentrated on the job of managers and the assumptions that they commonly make about people.

McGregor: The job of a manager[2]

As McGregor saw it, the way a manager does his job is based upon his view of people and their behaviour. He distinguished two sorts of view of human nature and behaviour, 'Theory X' and 'Theory Y' – indeed it might even be said that he over-distinguished for the sake of clarity. Most managerial policy and practice, said McGregor, reflects the view of human nature and behaviour that he calls Theory X:

(i) Most people dislike work and avoid it if they can.

(ii) Because they inherently dislike work most people must be controlled, directed and threatened with some kind of punishment if they are to work hard enough to suit the organization.

(iii) Most people lack ambition, avoid responsibility, yearn for security and welcome being directed.

A manager who takes broadly this view of human nature and behaviour will see his job essentially as supplying the motivation that gets people to make an effort; directing their efforts; controlling what they do and making sure that it fits in with what the organization wants. The manager's authority is the indispensable means by which he maintains such control. He need not do this viciously or nastily. He may treat his subordinates equitably and his relations with them may be reasonable and pleasant much of the time. But the point is, said McGregor, that common though it be, this way of managing is not very effective for the organization. In fact it creates its own problems. The danger is that because they are treated as basically lazy and irresponsible, people will come to behave as if they are lazy and irresponsible. This behaviour then reinforces the manager's view and so a self-fulfilling prophecy is set up.

A Theory X view may be appropriate for the way some people behave at work some of the time, but, said McGregor, most people are not like this and will work better if managed in a different way. So he put forward another view of the manager's job, based on another way of looking at human nature and behaviour, which he called Theory Y, whose basic assumptions are:

(i) People want to work just as naturally as they went to rest or play. Under the right conditions work can be a source of great satisfaction. People will only avoid it if it is organized in a way that frustrates them.

(ii) If a person takes pride in his job he will motivate and control himself. Imposed control and threat of punishment are only necessary if this sense of pride is lacking.

(iii) Pride in a job and commitment to doing it well depend upon what a person feels he gets out of the job. The most significant rewards are not financial, but, rather, the satisfaction of needs for self-respect and self-fulfilment. It should be perfectly possible to find these rewards in doing a good job for the organization.

(iv) When a person takes pride in his job he gladly accepts, even seeks responsibility. Lack of ambition, the avoidance of responsibility and the overriding desire for security usually occur only when a person sees his job as an affront to his self-respect.

(v) The ability to use initiative and imagination in solving work problems is not confined to a few high-calibre people. It is potentially there in most people – production-line workers and clerks as well as managers. It just needs to be brought out.

(vi) The way most work is organized and managed taps only a small proportion of the average person's potential.

This view of human nature is also self-fulfilling. Because people are trusted and given scope they will work hard and use their experience and initiative constructively for the good of the organization.

Theory Y has quite different implications for managers than does Theory X. It implies that managers must constantly review the way they manage, adapting it to make the most of the people they have available at any given time. Above all, such managers must use their ingenuity to find new ways of enabling their subordinates to use and develop their abilities. If things seem to be going wrong, managers must beware of laying the blame on the laziness, indifference, irresponsibility or intransigeance of their subordinates since this would lead to the introduction of more rigorous controls to ensure adequate effort. Instead managers must ask where they themselves are going wrong, what more they could do to release the potential for development and the capacity to take responsibility inherent in each of the individuals with whom they work. This does not mean that managers should be soft on their people – rather that they be honest with themselves.

The important feature of Theory Y is not managerial authority, but what McGregor called 'integration'. By this he meant that managers should create the conditions which enable people to satisfy their own needs best by working hard for the success of their organization. Thus the goals of the individual and the organization would be naturally 'integrated' – a state which could never flow naturally from Theory X, but could only be approximated by direction and control. (Organizations which achieve integration of this kind have since been termed 'Theory Z' organizations, or 'hierarchical clans' by William Ouchi,[3] who maintains that they represent America's best hope of meeting Japanese competition.)

All this poses quite a challenge to managers. How might the challenge be successfully met and the potential benefits to individual and organization be realized? While the work of both Maslow and McGregor began to suggest the means it was the work of Frederick Herzberg that made these explicit.

Herzberg: How people react to their jobs[4]

Herzberg's distinctive contribution is that he focused attention on the importance of the nature of the jobs that people do, as contrasted with the conditions in which they do them. In an attempt to sort out some of the apparent contradictions in the work of behavioural scientists up to the late 1950s Herzberg and his colleagues went right back to basics. They put aside the theories and simply asked people to describe those times when they had felt particularly enthusiastic and satisfied at work and times when they had felt especially dissatisfied and frustrated.

Analysis of these descriptions showed that the causes of satisfaction and enthusiasm are different in kind from the causes of dissatisfaction and frustration. It is not, as is often supposed, that the presence of something causes satisfaction while its absence causes dissatisfaction. It seems that people derive lasting satisfaction almost entirely from factors to do with the nature, or content, of their work. The important aspects are the inherent interest, challenge and responsibility of the job and the opportunities it offers for personal achievement, development and self-respect. These are the factors that satisfy the 'higher-level' needs emphasized by Maslow. If present in his job they enable the individual to feel pride and enthusiasm and release the self-generated motivation and control that McGregor saw as the only reliable way of integrating the needs of the individual with those of his organization.

Because of this capacity to create willing effort Herzberg called these factors the 'motivators'. A job that lacks such aspects will not produce self-generated motivation.

On the other hand, dissatisfaction, Herzberg found, generally results from factors like the nature of company policy and administration, managerial and supervisory practices, human relationships, working conditions and the amount, security and system of pay – the 'context' rather than the content of the job. If people feel that they are poorly or inadequately treated in these respects they tend to feel dissatisfied and frustrated. If, by contrast, they feel they are well paid, well managed and work in pleasant conditions they feel only the absence of such frustrations. They do not feel positive satisfaction. They may not give trouble, but neither will they be motivated to give of their best. Good working conditions can only satisfy our 'lower-level' needs in Maslow's terms. In McGregor's terms, we may go on doing the job, but our boss will have to go on using the stick and the carrot to ensure we make the minimum effort required by the organization.

Because these two sets of factors are independent of each other there can be, as we know from experience, responsible people with a pride in their work who are dissatisfied with their working conditions. Nurses, doctors, firemen and teachers are typical examples. No matter how strong the sense of vocation and professional pride it does not remove the dissatisfaction caused by poor pay and conditions.

Equally, there are people who feel apathetic, even resentful, but who, for the time being at least, are not dissatisfied with their conditions. Workers on a car production line who have just achieved a pay rise might be an example. No matter how good the pay and conditions may be, they cannot adequately compensate for work that is monotonous and lacking in challenge. To try and compensate for it increases the cost of the problem but reduces the prospect of a solution. Because good working conditions only prevent trouble rather than result in something more positive, Herzberg referred to factors relating to job context as the 'hygiene factors'. His analogy was medical. Good hygiene helps prevent disease; it cannot positively generate health.

Whatever their limitations, these theories are useful in practice. They remind us that people are still people when they go to work; that people need to find enjoyment and pride in their work as well as in their leisure; and that they need this as well as, not instead of, fair pay and good conditions. These ideas are not an exhortation to managers to put aside normal business criteria like profit and simply treat people well. Nor do they justify the exploitation of an employee's natural sense of responsibility for the good of the organization alone. What these ideas do suggest is that it is quite possible to meet simultaneously the needs of employee, organization and customer; that this is the only business-like approach in the longer term; and that its success depends on trying as far as possible to shape jobs so that as well as providing decent pay and conditions, they offer scope for people to develop their skills and use their initiative. In the competitive and unpredictable world of today an organization needs its employees to contribute as much as they can.

Securing these potential benefits may entail a new way of thinking for some managers – and for some trade unionists. Both may have to think more widely. Managers may have to look beyond pay and conditions if they are to release enthusiastic effort. Trade unionists may have to widen the ambit of their representation to further their members' interests by becoming involved in decisions about job content and working methods as well as with pay and conditions. This broadening of horizons would give the opportunity for new forms of industrial relations.

All this offers a challenge to managers and trade unionists. As we have seen, traditional forms of managerial control are unlikely to be effective. But these theories by no means imply that control and authority be discarded in favour of committee rule and anarchy, rather that more appropriate methods of control be adopted, based on co-operation and earned respect instead of compulsion. And just as it is not enough for managers merely to direct in an authoritarian way, so it is not enough for trade union leaders simply to tell their members what is good for them. While some members may need help in formulating and expressing their ideas, they will still expect these ideas to be taken into account.

It can be gruelling for people to embark on such changes of attitude and practice even when they believe the change to be necessary. So why should they bother? After all the old ideas must have held good in the past or they would not have gained such a strong hold. It is true that some will want to make the effort because they feel it is justified morally and this conviction can lend them strength to face difficulties. But there is more to it than the moral argument, as the theories themselves suggest. Human nature may have stayed much the same since the industrialized world began, but social and economic conditions have changed drastically and this has influenced the way people behave at work.

It is worth trying to unravel some of these social changes because they have led to changes in people's behaviour, and these in turn have called for a parallel response from organizations.

Social and economic change

It is notoriously difficult to understand the recent past. For one thing we are inextricably bound up in it. For another, the change experienced in the last few decades has been both fundamental and particularly rapid. Thus any analysis is likely to be riddled with problems of perspective.

Nevertheless some facts stand out, even in the roughest analysis. To begin, we can examine the case of Britain where, despite the decline in wealth relative to other industrial nations, the standard of living of most people has improved dramatically since the Second World War. Of course, there is still poverty, but even standards of what constitutes poverty have changed. Most people are far better off than ever before. A higher standard of living means more comfortable, better-equipped homes, more to eat and drink and a wider range of things to do in our leisure.

But a higher standard of living means more than material improvement. By watching television, going out in the family car and by travelling abroad for our holidays, our experience is broadened and we become better informed. And for most people these already high expectations have, so far, gone on rising. Add to these improvements the greater sense of security offered by the development of the Welfare State, reinforced for trade union members by the growth of their power, and we have, in Maslow's terms, a society in which most of our basic needs are catered for for most of the time. By and large even though tragically large numbers are unemployed, the majority of people are more free than ever before to concern themselves with things less basic than earning a living.

Linked with this there have been some important changes in our education system. We are now able to educate more of our children for longer than ever before. And, perhaps even more significant to employers, we are also beginning to educate them differently. Previously the teacher's job was to teach children the specific knowledge that they were thought to need. Formal methods like rote-learning were common – most of us can remember reciting multiplication tables. Examinations and other checks on visible progress were frequent. With the exception of the occasional school trip, learning took place almost exclusively in the classroom, with the teacher, a figure of considerable authority, in the centre. Parents had little say in what went on and the children even less.

Recently this picture has been changing. The need for formal knowledge is now seen as less relevant to our changing world than the more practical ability of using information in innovation. New technology offers us sophisticated information retrieval systems. We need people who can put them to good use.

Together with this change in emphasis, the growing interest in the individual and his rights, particularly in his right to participate, has had its effect on the thinking of those involved in education, whether as teachers, administrators, parents or even children. The outcome is a move towards putting the children, rather than the teacher, at the centre of things. So-called 'discovery' methods are replacing more formal methods, taking learning out of the classroom and into the community. And methods of assessment are changing along with this. The 1980 Education Act made provision for parents to become more involved in governing schools and in some cases the children too are offered a part to play.

There are also similar trends in the way children are brought up by their parents. Emphasis is less on discipline, routine and parental authority and more on the needs of the individual child.

At their best these methods are producing well-rounded, self-reliant, innovative people willing to play their part and give of their best. They demand a response from employers because most existing jobs, managerial and specialist, as well as jobs on the shop floor or in the office, are structured too rigidly to allow such people the scope they require.

But mostly the new methods fall short of the ideal. Change in fundamental aspects of our lives, like education and upbringing, does not tend to proceed smoothly along clearly defined paths. Many contend that the new methods leave much to be desired. The news media report lower than acceptable standards of literacy and numeracy. Some parents and employers complain of a lack of respect and an unwillingness to make the disciplined effort necessary for success. Confusion – amongst teachers and children – is more apparent than the innovative confidence that forward-thinking educationalists are seeking.

The move towards learning which is based on discovery methods and centred on the individual child means quite an upheaval for teachers. Like those in other professions, teachers have been accustomed to a well-defined and respected position of authority. The new methods encourage children to question, learn and decide for themselves. Teachers no longer have the authority which comes from being those who 'know' – at least not to the same extent as when it was their job directly to pass on knowledge. And because the children are being taught to question the teacher's authority (and, outside school, that of the parents), that of the boss is being questioned too.

In an ideal world perhaps this might all proceed smoothly. Confident in their new role of 'resource' to the children, teachers would support and encourage children in their voyage of discovery and would earn the respect on which a new form of authority could be based. But the real world is far more ambiguous and attitudes change only very slowly. Many teachers are uneasy. Inevitably they communicate this to the children, some deliberately and others unconsciously by the way they behave.

On top of this there is further confusion. Imagination, innovation and discovery are all very well, but in the end employers still want to know what examinations a prospective employee has passed. So, formal examinations remain a strong influence on school life but they are now confusingly out of keeping with some of its other aspects. You have to make the 'appropriate' discoveries if you are going to get on.

From the employer's point of view the outcome of all this is that young people start work with contradictory attitudes to authority, to using their initiative and to participating in decision-making. Like those who have taught them and brought them up, the young are no longer sure of their own position. They have not been taught to obey without question, but they have not been taught self-discipline either. They are not sure if they are meant to be thinking for themselves, or whether they are supposed to be doing as they are told. So they go halfway. They are critical, but more often in a negative than in a positive sense. In questioning existing arrangements they ask, 'why should I do it?' rather than the more constructive question, 'how can this job best be done?' Their confusion leads them to ask defensively, 'what do I get out of it?' rather than to ask more confidently, 'what can I put into it?' They are wary of taking their part in decision-making because they suspect that there is someone else somewhere who is going to decide in the end anyway.

At its most dramatic, the effect of these changes is that increasing numbers of people are deciding that the world of work, as most of us know it, is just not good enough for them. We have all heard about executives who decide that the rat-race, however well paid, exacts too high a price in terms of the quality of life and who opt instead for running a small-holding, a cottage industry or self-employment of some kind. Similarly we have heard of students who work hard for their qualifications and then decide that it is a waste to use them in the world of work.

And this kind of concern is not confined to middle-class intellectuals. As the co-existence of labour shortages with high unemployment shows, increasing numbers of 'working class' people with only a basic education prefer the dole queue to the job which they feel wastes their time and abilities. Some of them may be 'work-shy scroungers', but many more are just trying to hang on to their freedom in the only way they feel is open.

Of course, though they grow in number, those who reject the world of work are relatively few. It may be well worth an employer asking why such people have made this choice, but his main concern is with the vast majority who go on working – turning up late irritatingly often perhaps, going off sick more than seems justified, but turning up none the less. The behaviour of these people has also been affected by the same profound social changes.

To put it crudely, people at work no longer behave like a commodity. Previously it seems that fear of losing the job that supported self and family was sufficient to ensure that people worked hard and uncritically. Most people apparently adapted gratefully to whatever job was available to them and hoped for little more than to continue to hold it down. They had little energy left to question whether or not the job was sufficiently stimulating or whether they were treated as responsible adults.

Employers did not have to occupy themselves with questions of discipline or motivation to the same extent as they do today. They could even think of reducing wages at times – though not with impunity, as the General Strike of 1926 demonstrated.

It is not like that now. Even in times of tragically high unemployment, such as we have encountered in the early 1980s, most people who have jobs do not worry so much about keeping them that they will behave compliantly and uncritically while doing those jobs. Perhaps affluence has become so much of a habit that we cannot remember how to fear poverty. Or, more likely, the time has simply passed (if indeed it ever existed) when people will work on, apparently unaffected by the nature of what they are asked to do and how they are asked to do it.

Some say that this attitude will revert as persistent high inflation and unemployment bite deeper and they point to the decreasing lateness and the falling rates of absenteeism of the early 1980s as evidence that this change is actually taking place. But in practice the clock can never be turned back. Situations never wholly revert – they evolve. And over the years several aspects of the unemployment situation have changed markedly. For instance, legislation and trade union power offer protection from some of the insecurities that were previously commonplace. And if all else fails there is always unemployment benefit and supplementary benefit to help people to manage. Add to this basic security the growing conviction that the individual and his wish to make something of his life really matter and we have a workforce that is less compliant than ever before.

Therefore, even if the sharpness of people's reactions to dull jobs has been softened as the value of having a job at all has increased, the problems created for employers by such jobs have not gone away. A decrease in absenteeism and lateness, useful though it is, is not of the same value to an employer as a positive increase in enthusiasm. It is the enthusiasm that employers need to help them survive in difficult times and to help them take advantage of any upturn.

Thus employers throughout the Western world have to concern themselves with questions of motivation. They can no longer look to their employees' desire for job security and money to manage the situation for them. So whatever the imperfections of the new educational methods, it is still important for employers to take their effects into account because people starting work today are behaving differently from the way that employees did in the past. Many managers see this and have adapted themselves, trying to find ways of making the most of the new potential offered by people educated by these methods. But there are more who either do not recognize the need to adapt, or else resist new methods for fear of the chaos that may result.

The danger with any analysis of social change is that it oversimplifies. In attempting to clarify the complexities it overlooks many events that are confusing and can be contradictory. One is left asking why more people do not just go ahead and take the action necessary to alleviate their difficulties. But it is always easier to analyse a situation than to deal with it. Analysis takes away the emotion and confusion – and it is emotion and confusion that make a situation difficult.

In any case managers and trade unionists faced with the impact of change on their organizations cannot just sit back and analyse. They have to take decisions. While considering what to do they see much that is apparently contradictory. For instance, they see some people demanding the chance to decide things for themselves, yet on other occasions refusing to take the simplest initiative; others pressing for improvements, but at the same time resisting change; seeking responsibility, but simultaneously behaving irresponsibly.

Perhaps at bottom it is the confusion surrounding pay that blurs the issue most and makes it hardest for managers and trade unionists to come to terms with the need to adapt to changing employee attitudes. The trouble is that pay and payment systems look like straightforward economic matters. They are not. We might expect others to be 'reasonable' about their pay, but we are certainly emotional about our own. We might expect others to work harder and with greater compliance after a pay rise, but we do not necessarily behave this way ourselves.

Attitudes towards money are a mixture of the rational and the emotional. The mix varies with the individual and changes all the time. Our view of what is reasonable and fair is based on many factors: for instance, what we need; what we would like to have; what we think others are getting; what we feel our employer can afford to pay; and how we feel about our job. None of these things can be determined objectively. So emotions – our own and those of others – are inevitably part of pay determination. And the less working people behave as a commodity, the more this matters.

As far as 'need' is concerned, we have in developed economies largely gone past the point, for the time being at least, where pay is determined by need. So much so that I doubt if we could even sensibly begin to define it. But 'need' must still be taken into account because in times of high and persistent inflation the cost of meeting basic needs – whatever these are seen to be – goes on increasing.

Discussions get more involved over questions of what people

would like to have as compared with what they need. It is very difficult to separate the two, especially if you are the person doing the wanting. For most people in our consumer society yesterday's aspirations are today's wants and tomorrow's expectations, even in times of high unemployment. It is fruitless to ponder whether or not people really need things like colour televisions, cars and holidays abroad. The fact is that many people have come to expect such things and it is these expectations that will influence their idea of what constitutes 'fair pay'. And if the cost of such items, and of whatever else is next on their list, goes up then, very likely, so will their idea of what is fair pay.

From this it does not follow that an organization should pay people whatever they want to meet their ever-escalating expectations. But it helps if those involved in pay negotiation recognize what is going on under the surface and feel for the expectations of others some of the sympathy that they feel for their own. This is easier said than done. One thing that makes it difficult is that it often appears that expectations and aspirations are related to tangible things like cars, colour televisions, larger homes and so on. To an extent, of course, they are. People enjoy watching colour television, travelling by car and living in pleasant surroundings. They want these things as such and so they want the money that buys them. But often what is most keenly wanted is least apparent, as the theories reviewed suggest. As well as being the means of acquiring the tangible, money can represent the means of acquiring the intangible: power, prestige or peace of mind. So it can symbolize whatever is important to an individual; whatever he wants to experience or achieve inside as well as outside work.

Thus the person who does not find his job satisfying may well be asking for more money for reasons which are anything but financial. He will try to make up for his lack of satisfaction in other ways. As we have seen, he may seek the status conferred by consumer durables. Or he may try to establish a degree of control by deliberate manipulation of the payment system – if it is one that gives him the opportunity.

These are things that most organizations expect and are prepared to handle. But it is unlikely that such things will be the only outlet for the frustrations of the under-utilized employee. More important is that he will go on wanting what he really lacks – the chance to develop as a human being while he is at work; to experience the excitement and fulfilment that only this offers; and to have a degree of control over matters that affect him. However much his organization pays him it will not be able to buy off such needs. Nor will it be able to buy his initiative and the imaginative, conscientious effort that people put into jobs that do justice to their abilities.

So, however high the price becomes, the individual will go on being dissatisfied; the organization will go on being troubled by his indifference, apathy or worse still by quality problems, restrictive practices and even by strikes; and customers will go on being faced with standards of goods and services below what they could be.

What stands out is that nowadays very few people can be reliably motivated to work hard by money – except perhaps in the very short term; and the short term is not long enough for most organizations. There may appear to be all sorts of exceptions to this dogmatic statement: the hard-driving salesman; the dedicated entrepreneur; the girl on the factory line who earns top bonus week after week. But is it really just money that has engaged their efforts? Perhaps the salesman enjoys the challenges of selling. Perhaps the entrepreneur really values the control over his own destiny that his business offers him. Perhaps the girl enjoys using her dexterity and ability to co-ordinate hand and eye.

However, the fact that money may no longer reliably stimulate effort need not be a matter for regret. Certainly it does mean that to understand pay and payment systems we have to try to understand some of the most confusing aspects of human nature – and we have to try to adapt traditional bargaining methods to take account of this. But, daunting and risky though this may be, it is what realism requires. And realism is a more secure basis for the future than sticking to an apparently simpler, but no longer relevant approach.

The key lies in ceasing to regard pay as the only reward that people expect to get out of their jobs, the only way of motivating them. Instead we have to pay attention to everything which encourages willing effort and makes it possible for people to use their initiative and experience not just day by day in their jobs, but in shaping their organization's response to the changing world in which it operates. Felt-fair pay and decent working conditions, which include an element of job security, will always be important as the framework. But the real stimulus comes from having work which provides interest, challenge and scope and the kind of managers who, far from resisting change, treat people as adults, encouraging them to develop their skills and use them to help their organization act responsively. The more organizations can provide working experience of this kind the more they will be in tune with their employees' needs; the better use will they be able to make of their employees' abilities; and the better equipped they will be to go on satisfying their customers in the changing world around them.

3 Attempts at improvement

As long as there have been organizations there have been people trying to help them to work better. The techniques used have altered considerably over time as economic, social and political circumstances have changed and as understanding of people's behaviour at work has grown. Today there is an almost bewildering variety of different approaches available, some of which seem to be complementary; some of which are apparently contradictory; and many of which seem to change almost as fashion dictates. This can be confusing to the manager or trade unionist who is trying to decide what to do. The aim of this chapter is to make some sense out of this confusion. To help make the picture clearer let us look first at some of those techniques used in the recent past which have been most influential.

The 'hard' approach

The earliest attempts to help organizations to work more effectively took what is often called the 'hard' approach. One of the first change strategies to be widely applied, and certainly the one which has influenced subsequent developments most, was that introduced in the early years of this century by Frederick Winslow Taylor[1] and known as 'scientific management'.

The expressed objective of scientific management was to achieve maximum prosperity for both employer and employee. It required both managers and workers to go through what Taylor saw as a 'mental revolution'. Instead of wasting energy in arguing about the division of the company surplus between dividends and pay they should work together to ensure that this surplus should be as large as possible. By pulling together instead of against each other they would, in Taylor's opinion, find that the surplus was great enough to allow both large wage increases and large increases in dividends.

A strictly rational system was applied to ensure this increase in productivity. Exact knowledge was substituted for guesswork and judgement. Jobs were broken down into their simplest component elements and the time taken to perform each element was rigorously established and recorded. From this data, pay rates could be set for each job. The aim was that employees would be scientifically selected for jobs and trained to be able to work with maximum efficiency on the highest grade of work of which they were thought to be capable. It was intended that they should be given this kind of work to do whenever possible. The high earnings they could thus obtain would, in Taylor's view, motivate them to perform at their peak.

Taylor's system aroused a good deal of interest and hope at the time. Now it is fashionable almost to belittle him, in particular for the intensity of his belief in the power of money to motivate and for the unskilled, repetitive tasks his system created. But these criticisms, valid though they may be, are being made eighty years or more after Taylor's time with all the benefit of hindsight. What was being said by his contemporaries is perhaps more telling. Widespread though the application of Taylor's ideas was, the approach was bitterly resisted by some of those upon whom it was imposed. Machines were broken in protest and Taylor himself was threatened with violence. The trade unions felt it intensified industrial unrest. They saw it as anti-union and undemocratic, and claimed that it exploited the workers and condemned them to a monotonous routine.

Taylor's approach was also criticized by contemporary researchers, notably R. F. Hoxie,[2] who prepared a report on scientific management for the United States Commission on Industrial Relations in 1915. Hoxie reported that scientific management had undoubtedly produced some economic benefits but, he said, these benefits were counteracted by less welcome results. Some of these could be attributed to fake experts jumping on to Taylor's bandwagon and misapplying his ideas. But Hoxie's criticism went deeper. He doubted whether it was possible to be as rational and scientific about human affairs as Taylor claimed. Taylor was an idealist who did not distinguish between what looks possible in theory and what can be done in practice.

The most telling criticism made by Hoxie was that most of those applying scientific management did not recognize the humanitarian and social problems they were creating, nor that these problems were undermining any potential economic benefits. The practitioners seemed ignorant of the findings of contemporary economists and social scientists. The problem posed for the practitioners and companies using the system was to find a way of retaining the economic benefits while reversing the social and psychological damage caused.

Hoxie's report apparently had little impact at the time, but it has proved to be prophetic. We can see now how this kind of approach creates the problems which undermine the high productivity that it seeks to create. Because their non-monetary needs are disregarded, workers in the de-skilled, tedious jobs resort to all manner of unproductive activities ranging from lax performance to sabotage. They are late, sick or absent. They change jobs frequently, thereby involving their company in the expense of training their replacements – one of the expenses that Taylor's system was intended to reduce. And, because the structure of their jobs deprives them of influence, they seek to establish control unofficially through whatever loopholes they can find, from manipulation of time measurement and pay systems to the deliberate restriction of output.

But despite all these criticisms Taylor's ideas and what has sprung from them have had, and continue to have, enormous influence. The use of assembly lines and other highly systematic processes in both offices and factories are in line with Taylor's ideas and so too is work study. Many jobs, whether clerical, manual or even managerial, have been designed to be as specialized and standardized as possible, which is perfectly consistent with Taylor's thinking. In addition, many control systems are based on Taylor's assumption that all aspects of human performance can be reliably costed and measured.

In view of the evident shortcomings of such methods we need to find the answers to certain questions. For instance, why have the ideas on which they are based persisted for so long? Why have attempts to deal with the problems thus created so often consisted of yet more rigorous application of the same ideas? If high labour turnover is caused by boring jobs, why does the remedy so often take the form of further de-skilling? And why are the efforts of the clerk to get round a rigid system and make it work so often met with further over-specification? Why, in effect, are the real causes of such difficulties so seldom recognized?

Part of the answer to this kind of question seems to lie in the emotional appeal of these apparently rational ideas. The prospect they offer of high productivity and low-cost training is very important, but I do not think that this is where the strength of their appeal lies. Emotionally they hold out to managers the hope of making the unpredictable predictable and of controlling the uncontrollable. These are the aspects of their jobs with which managers find it most difficult to cope, and the same is true of trade union representatives and advisers.

We may know that the prospect of control is illusory, that unpredictability is inevitable and must eventually be accepted, but such knowledge does not stop us from yearning for control and certainty. Nor does it prevent us from preferring methods which suggest that control is possible to those which force us to accept unpredictability. We prefer to behave irrationally, while calling our behaviour rational.

Ironically, it seems that the so-called 'soft' approach, the followers of which are frequently criticized for their irrationality, is in many ways more realistic about human behaviour than what is regarded as the 'hard', rational approach.

The 'soft' approach

Briefly defined, the 'soft' approach is one which takes account of workers' feelings, beliefs and attitudes. It arose largely in reaction to the more mechanistic ideas of the 'hard' approach. The soft approach originated in the now famous Hawthorne Studies conducted by Elton Mayo[3] at the Western Electric Company's Hawthorne Works near Chicago between 1924 and 1932. The conclusion of this research was declared to be that people will be motivated to produce more if the human relations they experience at work satisfy their social and psychological needs. It now seems that the research itself contained little hard evidence to justify this conclusion. Nonetheless it became the underlying assumption of the 'human relations movement' which grew out of Mayo's research. This movement stimulated much subsequent work, particularly in the United States, but also elsewhere.

A new approach to organization change has grown out of this movement. It aims to increase efficiency by improving the ability of managers and supervisors to handle human relationships. Initially this was attempted through lectures on such topics as 'The Supervisor and his Study of Human Nature', 'Motivation', 'Attitudes', 'Opinions and Morale', and 'Psychological Aspects of Absenteeism and Turnover'. These lectures were supplemented by discussion of case studies and the learning acquired was often assessed by written tests.

However, it was often found that neither the morale nor the productivity of subordinates improved when their superiors were trained in this way. Efforts were made therefore to improve training methods. As a result training by means of lectures began to be replaced by learning in so-called 'T' or 'training groups' – a method common today. Basically this consists of a small number of people meeting over a period of time with a trainer whose task is to encourage them to examine their own behaviour and what goes on in the group. There is usually no defined structure: the aim is that people will learn directly from their 'here and now' experience of what happens in the group.

Even with these new training methods the effect on the morale and performance of subordinates has been disappointing. Certainly many of those who have undergone sensitivity training feel they have benefited personally, but apparently this personal benefit is seldom translated into benefit to the organization.

Some of the shortcomings of the human relations approach can undoubtedly be attributed to the ineptitude of some practitioners – as can the shortcomings of any approach. But ineptitude is not the basic problem. Powerful though it can be as a way of increasing people's awareness of their own behaviour and of what makes groups work effectively the method itself is inadequate as a means of changing organizations. Its crucial weakness is that it focuses only on human relationships, and these relationships, however good they may be, do not themselves determine whether or not an organization is successful. The key factors are the nature of production and control systems and the kind of jobs they create; training in human relations is not concerned with these and thus has no effect on them.

What typically happens in practice is that, as a result of the training, managers become more aware of their own behaviour and the effect that this has on others. In the training group they try out new ways of behaving and become more skilled at bringing out the best in others. They finish the training course determined to try to improve the morale and contribution of their subordinates and with high hopes of success. But when they get back to their jobs they find that their subordinates, their boss and even their colleagues fail to respond to their efforts to change things. Sooner or later this lack of response discourages them. All that remains is a private feeling of having been helped by the training at the time and a conviction that their efforts at improvement might have succeeded if only others were more sensitive.

Sometimes subordinates, boss and colleagues are trained too but even then the pattern tends to be the same. The benefit of the training is seldom transferred to normal operations. This is because the basic problem is not one of sensitivity, but of what is allowed by the nature of production and control systems, by the sort of jobs that people do. For instance, the most sensitive encouragement of subordinates to contribute new ideas will fail if the jobs those subordiantes do give them no scope to use their initiative. The subordinates are not being unresponsive: they are being realistic. In effect the organization is telling them clearly, through the way that their jobs are structured and their performance assessed, that initiative is discouraged rather than valued. They soon learn not to bang their heads on a brick wall.

So both the 'hard' and the 'soft' approach have serious short-comings as methods of improving the effectiveness of an organization. Put crudely, the 'hard' concentrates on task at the expense of people and the 'soft' on people while excluding consideration of the task. Neither looks at the relationship between what people are asked to do and how well they do it and, ultimately, it is on this relationship that the effectiveness of an organization depends.

There are, however, approaches to change which take this relationship into account. Research along these lines began as early as the 1920s, but it was not until the late 1940s that practical attempts to change organizations began to take shape, by which time the influence of the work of Maslow and others was beginning to clarify insights into the nature of people's needs. Many different approaches are in use today, each looking in a slightly different way at the relationship between people and the production system. The two which have been most used and which are most influential are job enrichment and the socio-technical approach.

Job enrichment

The approach to improving the effectiveness of organizations via job enrichment originated in the work of Frederick Herzberg (described in Chapter 2). Herzberg's contribution was that he stressed the importance of the nature of a person's work in stimulating the commitment that leads to good performance.

Job enrichment aims to increase people's motivation and therefore their efficiency by increasing their job satisfaction. To do so it deliberately builds into jobs greater scope to do interesting, challenging, responsible work and to experience the sense of achievement and recognition that this brings. Thus it changes jobs so that they give more opportunity to develop the skills which lead to advancement.

The exact form the process takes depends a good deal on the individual practitioner, but it usually consists of the following elements:

(i) Identifying the jobs where problems of motivation seem to be causing problems of performance. Symptoms might include high labour turnover and absenteeism, low morale, low productivity, indifference to quality, etc.

(ii) Analysing such jobs to determine how far their content already offers scope for doing interesting, responsible work and how far such scope might be increased.

(iii) Determining which specific improvements in job content might be introduced. Techniques for doing this vary, but frequently include 'brainstorming' – a process in which a group of people are invited to contribute ideas spontaneously, without at that time being asked to consider whether the ideas would work in practice. The composition of such groups varies. They might, for instance, include the line managers responsible for the job being enriched, personnel and other related support services, the internal and external advisers and trade union representatives. They might also include some of those who actually do the job, though this was discouraged by the earlier practitioners. Their argument was that the job holder was unlikely to be able to contribute the creative ideas on which real improvement depends because his or her imagination would be more restricted by the status quo than other possible contributors. This view was modified as interest in participation grew and as experience of using job enrichment in practice demonstrated that the commitment that comes from involvement can be at least as valuable as theoretically good ideas.

(iv) Evaluating the feasibility of the ideas for improvement and considering their relative advantages and disadvantages, from the motivational as well as the practical point of view. The specific changes to be introduced can then be selected. These usually cover the content of the job, the way the work is controlled and the feedback of information about how well the job is being done. Examples of typical changes which embody the 'motivators' identified by Herzberg are:

Opportunity for achievement: introduce more difficult tasks not previously handled, e.g. allow clerks to compose individual letters to customers, instead of using standard paragraphs.

Recognition for achievement: assign special tasks to individuals who then become 'experts', consulted by their colleagues; let people know how they are doing – praise good work, help people to see how their performance could be improved.

Increased responsibility: delegate decisions to the lowest level at which they can sensibly be taken; remove some checks, e.g. allow typists to check their work and send it directly to the client; make shop floor workers responsible for their own quality control; give managers full authority to spend within an agreed budget.

More interesting work: give more variety, e.g. to assemble a whole heater or radio instead of performing just one of the constituent tasks; allow individuals the opportunity to think and use their own discretion about how things should be done as well as actually to do things.

Personal growth and professional advancement: allow freedom to plan a whole job, giving the individual the chance to decide when to seek advice; pass down responsibility for looking after and developing others, e.g. allow clerks and shop floor workers to give some on-the-job training to new colleagues; allow craftsmen and technicians the opportunity of doing higher skilled work usually reserved for supervisors.

(v) Offering the changes as options. Occasionally such changes are introduced as a package. But in the more successful applications they tend to be offered as options, together with any training required. This has the advantage of enabling people to try out the new ways of working as and when they feel capable. The more skilled and adventurous may take up the opportunity relatively quickly. Those less able or less confident can wait until they are ready or, indeed, may decide to continue to work as before if they prefer, although in practice this is rare. Experience shows that the variety of working procedures that can result creates few serious problems – far fewer than forcing changes on the unwilling and unable.

(vi) Introducing the changes experimentally. Changes providing job enrichment are usually introduced for an experimental period to enable their effectiveness to be evaluated. One common way is for the 'before' and 'after' levels of job satisfaction and productivity in 'experimental' groups which adopt the changes to be compared with those of 'control' groups which continue to work as before. The experimental period must be long enough to enable people first to get used to the changes (during which time a drop in productivity is not unusual) and then for any ephemeral enthusiasm caused simply by the novelty of the new methods to wear off (while such enthusiasm lasts productivity often peaks unrealistically). It is quite common therefore to allow one year for an experimental period. Meanwhile the pay and conditions of both experimental and control groups ideally remains stable.

(vii) Evaluating results and deciding whether to use the technique more widely in the organization.

Job enrichment achieved a good deal of popularity in the late 1960s and early 1970s, particularly in the USA and in Great Britain. In the US the technique attracted political interest, and satisfaction at work was adopted by Edward Kennedy as one of the major issues of his 1976 presidential campaign. Pressure grew for compulsory introduction of job enrichment, largely because of the social costs of unenriched jobs.

The technique has been used to enrich a wide variety of factory, clerical and managerial jobs by many organizations all over the world. Examples include Philips Industries, Richard Baxendale, ICI, Shell UK Ltd, Dexion – Comino, Texas Instruments, Carrington Dewhurst, AT&T (USA), GLC, Ferranti, South Eastern Electricity Board, United Biscuits, Canadian Transport Terminals. Such work demonstrated that much could indeed be achieved by deliberately trying to improve the content of a job. The benefits such companies reported include:

increased sales,
greater productivity per person,
improved quality,
fewer levels of supervision needed,
lower absenteeism, labour turnover and sabotage,
increased flexibility of the workforce, especially on assembly lines and in clerical work,
increased job satisfaction and more commitment to doing a good job.

The most significant and well-documented work was carried out by Imperial Chemical Industries (ICI) in the UK, the American Telephone and Telegraph Company (AT&T) in the USA, and Philips Industries in the Netherlands. A wide variety of jobs were enriched in these organizations including those of sales representatives, scientists, foremen, clerical staff, technicians and shopfloor workers.[4] As well as helping many companies to alleviate practical difficulties, the use of job enrichment has also helped to clarify, both for jobs and organization, the principles of good design.

However, notwithstanding the good results that have been achieved by using it, job enrichment has also been heavily criticized. The most common criticisms of it can be divided roughly into three categories: those which reflect a misunderstanding of what job enrichment is and what it sets out to do; those which are really a comment on the shortcomings of the experimental approach; and more serious criticisms which point to genuine inadequacies in the technique itself.

1. *Misunderstandings*

(i) job enrichment has been confused with other techniques which do not seek to do the same thing and which have not achieved such good practical results. These are job enlargement, job rotation, and job redesign (also called work structuring) – all terms which are commonly, and wrongly, used interchangeably with job enrichment.

Neither job enlargement nor job rotation try in improve the motivational content of jobs (what is sometimes called 'vertical loading'). They both simply provide more tasks of the same motivational level ('horizontal loading'), either by increasing the number of tasks performed, as in the case of job enlargement, or by giving the individual a succession of similar tasks to do, as in the case of job rotation.

Unlike job enlargement and job rotation, work structuring does seem to improve the motivational content of jobs. However, it tends to replace one fixed job structure with another one equally fixed, albeit with more challenging content. The drawback is that the new fixed structure may provide too much challenge for some and insufficient for others. Thus the potential benefits of making the job more challenging are not always realized. Job enrichment, on the other hand, tends to offer the changes as options, rather than as new fixed requirements, thus enabling people to adopt the new possibilities when they feel able.

(ii) Enrichment of some jobs is sometimes said to lead inevitably to the impoverishment of others, particularly that of the line manager, or supervisor directly above. In practice this need not happen since all linked jobs can be enriched as part of the same programme. But in any case the feared impoverishment tends not to happen. Organizations usually report that the delegation of some supervisory functions, such as checking, actually frees the supervisor to do the higher level work for which his experience and ability equip him, work which his checking functions often prevent him from doing. The result is not impoverishment of the supervisor's job, but actually its enrichment – to the mutual benefit of supervisor and subordinate.

However, it is difficult to envisage this kind of change in the quality of a job and this difficulty contributes to a common fear of impoverishment, particularly amongst supervisors.

(iii) Job enrichment is sometimes said, particularly by trade unionists, to be a means of exploiting the workers by getting them to do more responsible work without a corresponding increase in pay. Certainly, improving productivity and quality are the chief motives managers have for introducing job enrichment. Like any technique, it can be misused, but exploitation is not inherent in the technique. While job holders undoubtedly benefit from intangible improvements such as increased job satisfaction, there is no need for the story to end there. Material benefits to the company can also be, and usually are, passed on to the workers.

2. *Weaknesses of the experimental approach*

As we have seen, changes designed to enrich jobs tend to be introduced in a small-scale, experimental way, rather than be immediately applied throughout an organization. Such experimentation enables the organization to monitor the effects of the changes in a relatively controlled and risk-free fashion. However, partial application can also present certain problems. Where these have been well handled no difficulties have arisen. Where they have not been so well handled the difficulties created have led to criticism of the technique itself. It is said:

(i) to take place on too small a scale to be of much benefit to the organization;

(ii) that the problems of extending any benefits from small-scale to large-scale implementation are overwhelming;

(iii) that the length of the experimental period – often about one year – causes problems because the experimental groups and the rest of the organization are out of step with each other. There may be difficulties in holding working conditions constant over such a long period. There may also be problems because people in the experimental group are taking more responsibility without higher pay over such a long period, particularly if they are then asked to abandon the changes and return to the former way of working. Some trade unionists fear that the consequences of this could seriously undermine their role in collective bargaining.

3. *Serious inadequacies*

Some of the criticisms of job enrichment are really the result of misunderstanding, or of the mishandling of the problems arising out of the experimental nature of the approach. However, there are other more serious criticisms which expose the ways in which job enrichment is inadequate as a means of changing organizations. For instance:

(i) Failure sufficiently to involve job holders and the trade unions. While there are some cases where involvement has been widespread (for example the later work carried out by ICI in introducing the Weekly Staff Agreement to its Gloucester nylon spinning plant: Daniel and McIntosh 1972), there are many more instances where practitioners' concern for the purity of their approach has meant little or no involvement of the job holder and where job enrichment projects have not been sufficiently integrated with the collective bargaining framework. (This latter factor has caused many trade unionists to suspect the technique as an attempt by management to undermine the legitimate role of the trade unions.)

(ii) Acceptance of technological constraints.
Job enrichment has generally been used to improve existing jobs where the technology or system is more or less fixed so, where existing technology does not impose constraints on change, the technique has a good deal of scope to bring about improvements. But where changes in the technology or system would mean expensive alterations it has been said that job enrichment too readily accepts the

constraints imposed and thus can bring about only limited improvement.

(iii) Over-concentration on job content.

By definition job enrichment seeks only to improve the content of the job. Important though this is there are other aspects of working life that might need complementary improvement if lasting benefits are to be achieved, such as pay, working conditions and standards of training and supervision. The technique does not seek to improve these. But to be effective in the longer term any approach to organizational change must bring about necessary improvements in these aspects too as part of an integrated approach.

The result of such criticisms is that job enrichment is seldom used now in anything like its original form, often being regarded as one of those outmoded techniques which has had its day. This is probably a reaction against the somewhat excessive popularity it once enjoyed, but it is not an accurate view of the contribution it has made. Inadequate though its pure form may be in current circumstances, its emphasis on job content pointed the way to the more flexible and participative approaches in use today. Indeed, its influence is apparent in less clearly defined, but widely used, approaches such as organization development and in certain forms of productivity bargaining, like that involving workers at the Esso refinery at Fawley, BP Tanker Drivers, TI Tubes production workers and British Oxygen depot staff. It has also been incorporated in the more enduring socio-technical approach.

The socio-technical approach

The socio-technical approach originated in research started by the Tavistock Institute of London during the late 1940s. Essentially this approach requires some kind of analysis of:

(i)   the technical system used to produce the goods or service,

(ii)   the social system, or the way people are organized when working on this system;

(iii) the effect that the technical and social systems have on each other.

The Tavistock research began by investigating the social and psychological effects of introducing a particular form of mechanization – the longwall method – into coal-mining. Mechanization had been introduced with the expectation of increasing productivity. The new technical system required changes in the way the miners were organized and in the way they related to each other. Previously the men had worked in small self-regulating teams, each man carrying out all the various component tasks of mining. The new system replaced these teams with larger groups of between forty and fifty men; each team carried out just one specialized task instead of the whole range. Each of these larger teams worked independently, in shifts. But because the tasks performed by each were interrelated the teams were actually dependent on each other to get the work done. Control and co-ordination of activity was imposed by higher authority outside the teams; it no longer came from the men themselves within the teams.

What happened was that each team took a short-term approach, trying to make the best use of conditions in its own interest, and thereby creating and passing on more difficult working conditions to the groups responsible for subsequent tasks. Thus the new system promoted competition and conflict instead of co-operation between teams and between individual men. Low standards tended to be blamed on to others and absenteeism was high. As a result the hoped-for increase in productivity was not achieved.

Further research found that the men, in conjunction with their union officials and pit managers, had sometimes spontaneously established autonomous groups and more cohesive ways of working in an effort to solve some of the problems that the new system had created. The autonomous groups both produced more and were more satisfactory to their members than were the groups conventionally established to use the new technology – even though the spontaneously formed autonomous groups were not always smaller. This finding demonstrated that the use of a particular technical system need not tie an organization to any one social system. There is a range of options.

The early work in British coal-mining showed the potential usefulness of the socio-technical approach in improving the way organizations worked. It did seem to offer advantages over both scientific management and the human relations approach. For instance, neither of these approaches could have explained or reduced the inter-group conflict engendered by the new working methods. Thus neither could promote the hoped-for productivity increase.

It would follow from the precepts of scientific management that since the technology was right and since the miners were motivated by a piece-rate wages system then productivity would automatically increase but, as we have seen, it did not. The human relations school would assume that the inter-group conflict could be reduced by making the miners more aware of their relationship with each other and with other groups. But since this relationship was obscured by the everyday demands of the required working methods, any awareness so created would be ephemeral.

However, the socio-technical approach clearly needed refinement before it could be accepted as a proven means of helping organizations. Subsequently it has been used in a variety of locations: for instance in factories, process industries and on board ships, and in countries such as Norway, the USA, Sweden, the Netherlands, Denmark, Israel and India. Despite these different settings the findings have been very similar and the results achieved have been useful in terms of improving both productivity and attitudes in a wide range of circumstances.

Applications of the socio-technical approach have always been strongly integrated with the theoretical research on which they are based: practice enriches theory and theory in turn enriches practice. As a result the great range of applications are well-documented[5] and the general concepts on which they are based have been clarified in a way not possible with other approaches to organization change.

The guiding concepts currently used are:

(i) if an organization follows the dictates of the technical system at the expense of the social (or the social at the expense of the technical) the good results hoped for will not be achieved;

(ii) for any one technical system a whole range of workable social systems is possible;

(iii) the use of cohesive, autonomous groups as the base of the social system offers great advantages in terms of the satisfaction and commitment of the workers and, therefore, in terms of productivity;

(iv) for best results it is preferable to design (or redesign) the technical and social systems together (originally the technical system is taken as given and the social system redesigned to give improved results, but more recently it has become clear that better results can be achieved if the technical system is improved, or chosen, in conjunction with the social system);

(v) an organization (or 'socio-technical system') cannot be isolated from the environment in which it operates (the so-called 'open-systems' approach); socio-technical analysis therefore now incorporates the relationship between an organization and its environment, taking into account how changes in the world of work affect society and how changes in society affect the world of work;

(vi) relevant trade unions should be fully involved in research and experimental projects and where possible the workers affected by changes should also have a say in their formulation (again this was not originally typical of the socio-technical approach, but recently its importance has become more apparent – possibly because a good deal of the more recent work has been done in Norway and Sweden with their national emphasis on industrial democracy and participation).

Like job enrichment, the socio-technical approach has also helped to clarify the criteria of good job design – good, that is, not just from a welfare or moral point of view, but good because it results in fuller use of people's abilities and in better performance. One project has contributed greatly to this clarification. It started in Norway in 1962 under the joint control of the Norwegian Confederation of Employers (NAF) and the Trade Union Congress of Norway (LO) with the aim of using autonomous groups as the basis for increasing the participation of workers in decision taking. The action-researchers working on the project listed the criteria as they identified them during the project, but the items on their list would not now be seriously challenged by any experienced researcher, even those not using the socio-technical frame of reference.

1. *General requirements*

Jobs should:

be reasonably varied and mentally demanding;
offer the opportunity to go on learning on the job;
allow people to take some decisions and use discretion;
enable people to support and be supported by their colleagues and to have their efforts recognized;
enable people to relate what they do at work to the objectives of the company and to feel that their job is consistent with their life outside work;
lead to some desirable future.

2. *Specific requirements*

A. From the individual point of view each job should:

offer the optimum variety of tasks – too much variety can cause training and production problems and can frustrate the worker; too little can cause boredom and fatigue: the optimum mix allows tasks which stimulate, as well as provide a break from high levels of effort and concentration;

hang together coherently – although the elements of a task should vary, these elements should fit together and relate sensibly to the end product; this enables the individual to work in the way he prefers as well as to relate his job to that of his colleagues;

offer the optimum length of work cycle – too short a cycle means that starting and finishing breaks up working rhythm; too long a cycle makes it hard to build up a working rhythm;

offer scope for setting standards of quantity and quality, plus feedback of results – management may well have to set minimum standards, but if they are to accept responsibility for improving standards the workers must also have some influence: they are more likely to learn to improve the way they work on the job if they are given information about how they are doing;

include some auxiliary and preparatory tasks – workers will not accept responsibility for matters beyond their control; the inclusion of auxiliary and preparatory jobs in their range of tasks extends the scope of their control and thus increases their commitment to doing the job well;

require something – care, skill, knowledge or effort – which is respected by the community;

make an obvious contribution towards producing what the customer wants or needs.

B. At the group level help can be provided by building in interlocking tasks, job rotation, or putting people together wherever:

jobs are necessarily independent (for technical or psychological reasons) – at a minimum this aids communication and helps create mutual understanding, thus reducing friction and recrimination, at best, it stimulates co-operation between groups;

jobs entail high stress – communication with others in similar situations helps reduce strain e.g. from noise, physical activity, isolation etc;

jobs do not obviously make a contribution to the final product.

C. Wherever jobs are linked together by interlocking tasks or job rotation they should together:

appear to be an overall task which makes a contribution to the final product;

provide scope for standard setting for the workers, as well as feedback of results;

allow some control over related tasks.

These criteria for well-designed jobs were never intended to be final. They are a good guide given the current state of understanding, but they may well be modified and refined as circumstances change, for instance as we get more experienced at involving workers and their trade unions in designing jobs and organizations.

The socio-technical approach is widely used today, particularly in Scandinavia, and in Israel, Australia and the USA and it continues to yield useful results. While it is not a panacea for all problems it has contributed greatly to the emergence of a new approach to improving the way that organizations work. This new approach is pragmatic and since it does not rely on any particular technique it cannot easily be labelled. It is beginning to be used by a variety of advisers like engineers and ergonomists as well as behavioural scientists and management consultants.

Its essence is helping people to help themselves. The focus is less on following theory and contributing to research, more on encouraging people to define their own operational problems and to design, try out and evaluate improvements for themselves and, in the process, to apply what they learn.

It means a new role for any professional advisers involved. Their experience is put to a different use. The adviser, once the 'expert' upon whose knowledge decisions about what to do were based, is now a catalyst, the outside stimulus that gets the process of change going and then provides the support and encouragement needed by those who are trying to do things for themselves. This is a far more difficult role, as those who work in this way can testify.

The guiding principle of this new approach is that something called 'the quality of working life' does indeed matter. It matters because organizations which provide poor working experience tend not to be successful. They waste the time and talents of the people they employ and this can lead them in turn to waste the time and money of their customers. They are neither equipped to survive in the hard, competitive times of today, nor to thrive in any economic upturn. In the end too many people suffer needlessly from this frustration and waste, psychologically as well as financially.

The second section of this book describes how certain prominent organizations have started to use some form of this new approach in order to survive or even flourish in today's rapidly changing circumstances.

PART II

Organizations at work

Introduction to the case studies

The first part of this book looked in general and theoretical terms at the way people work in organizations: where things go wrong and why, and what might be done to help. This second part looks at the same themes, but in practical terms. It describes what several prominent organizations have done to improve the way they function by coming to grips with these problems. These case studies illustrate the kind of problems organizations are facing, different attempts to cope with such problems, and the results of these attempts. The cases described are taken from:

(i) the car manufacturing industry in Europe and the USA,
(ii) the Italian metal working industry,
(iii) the British Civil Service.

The cases chosen are only examples and do not incorporate the whole of European and North American motor manufacturing, the whole of the Italian metal working sector, nor even the whole of the British Civil Service. They can only begin to give a flavour to the work being done by thousands of organizations in industry, commerce and government all over the world. Despite this inevitable limitation they are in many ways representative.

They illustrate the situation in a wide range of different organizations in both public and private sectors in the UK and abroad; they cover offices and factories, service, production and process industries. They include large, well-known organizations like Volvo, Olivetti and many of the major departments of the British Civil Service, as well as smaller units for comparison.

All the organizations included are taking a radical approach and asking themselves some basic questions, rather than just tinkering with cosmetic changes. They are all working on important issues like the effect on an organization of changes in customers' requirements; the introduction of new technology into offices and factories; the impact of changing attitudes among employees and increased trade union militancy; the meaning of industrial democracy and employee participation in practical terms; and the roles of management, of trade unions, and of advisers.

Perhaps because the organizations concerned are attempting radical changes the case studies are not all unqualified success stories. Mistakes have been made and the cases show how people have built upon the lessons learned from them. Another reason for choosing these particular cases is that they are taken from those of which I have direct knowledge. This personal involvement offers a more secure basis from which to draw conclusions and make comparisons than does reliance on second-hand reports.

One thing that the case studies do not represent is the Japanese way of working. This is not because I think we have little to learn from the Japanese. On the contrary, the success of their enterprise alone makes it essential for us to consider the way they operate, and there is much worth considering in the efficiency of their training, the excellence of their internal communications, and the readiness of their managers to discuss matters with their subordinates. In Japanese companies in Japan and elsewhere the involvement of employees in matters affecting their own work is a deliberate management policy because it is profitable. There is a good deal to be learnt from this. Indeed, as the great interest aroused by the work of people like William Ouchi demonstrates, we have already begun to consider and learn from it. But learning from what people in another culture do is not straightforward, particularly when the issues are complex and emotive and the cultures as different as our own from that of Japan where, in spite of recent social change, subordination of the individual to the family, the team at work, the company and the society is still far more culturally ingrained than in Western industrial nations like the UK and USA.

Nothing illustrates the difficulties of learning from Japan more clearly than the 'quality circles' movement that we have seen in the early 1980s. In Japan 'quality circles' have become an integral part of a total system supported by a coherent management philosophy. Too many organizations in the West have selected this apparently simple and easily implemented idea as a panacea for all their ills without examining or understanding the total system of which it is but a small part.

The effective management of human resources is a complex task; helping people to examine the subtleties involved and to be responsive to the circumstances in which they operate is therefore difficult. Since to introduce the extra dimension of deep cultural differences would only add further complications, I have taken my examples from cases which do not suffer from this disadvantage. [1]

To facilitate comparison the three case studies that follow will be presented under these five headings:

1. Background.
2. The problems faced.
3. The changes made.
4. How the changes were made.
5. What happened as a result.

4 The motor manufacturing industry

1. Background

For many people, motor manufacturing epitomizes mass production industry. The car assembly line, pioneered by Henry Ford in the days of scientific management, represented all that was seen as being good and efficient in modern manufacturing methods. Recently, as our ideas and expectations have changed, assembly lines in car factories have for many people come to symbolize all that is bad. Since the early 1960s something of a revolution has been taking place in car manufacturing methods in the Western World. Why this revolution came about, the form that it took and what happened as a result is a story of great significance to anyone, in office or factory, whose job it is to meet consumers' needs in today's competitive world.

This case study should put right a few widespread but dangerous misconceptions: that treating people decently is a luxury that companies can only afford when they have money to spare, or when times are easy; that it is something for soft-hearted organizations, but not for those which are hard-headed; that it is only possible where you do not have expensive technology already in place.

What the motor manufacturing industry demonstrates is that it is not necessary to treat people like bits of machinery in order to make a profit out of mass production. Indeed, some leading car manufacturers would go further and say that it is no longer possible to make a profit if you do treat people like bits of machinery. Treating people as people, and attending to their need to find satisfaction in their work, is just as important in bad times as it is in good times – in fact more so, because without releasing the know-how and the wholehearted effort of their workers many companies will fail to achieve the flexibility in production they need to survive, let alone thrive.

This case study incorporates the experience of several major manufacturers in Western Europe and North America. It concentrates on those who have been modifying the way work is organized at the same time as changing technology and production engineering systems – that is on those manufacturers where the impact of change on the working life of employees has probably been greatest. Not all manufacturers have adopted such a strategy. Ford (Europe), for instance, have concentrated on using ergonomics and improving industrial engineering systems, a somewhat different approach from that of the manufacturers included in this case study.

The paths taken by the manufacturers whose experience is included here (Volvo, Saab, Renault, Fiat, General Motors (USA) and certain prominent West German manufacturers, like BMW and Daimler Benz) differ markedly from each other, for a variety of operational and cultural reasons. Each of them was aiming to do what appeared best in the light of their own particular circumstances. But despite these important differences there are many common factors ranging from the reasons they had for taking action, to what happened as a result.

2. The problems faced

The reasons an organization has for changing the way it operates are crucial in determining the amount of effort that it will put into those changes, particularly when the going gets tough. One important reason stems from the economic background. Since the mid–1970s, the worsening world economic situation has caused a slump in demand which has led to a crisis in car production shared by virtually all manufacturers with the exception of some in Japan. The effect of this declining demand has been accentuated by changes in the type of product that customers want. The world energy crisis has led to an increased demand for smaller, more economical cars and growing concern with protecting the environment has led to pressure to save raw materials and to the introduction of legal requirements to reduce pollution and noise. Customers also increasingly require higher safety specifications, longer service intervals, and greater reliability and ease of maintenance.

Tastes have changed too. People are no longer willing to accept 'any colour as long as it's black', as they were in the early days of Henry Ford. They now expect a good colour range and a wide variety of attractive interiors – all at a relatively low overall cost. None of this remains static. Customers' requirements go on changing, so that manufacturers who wish to remain competitive need to revise their models constantly. This means reviewing design and production methods as well as the product itself. Indeed, being responsive to changing demands of customers in the context of a shrinking and fiercely competitive market increasingly means designing the product and the manufacturing process together.

The technological advances of the 1960s and 1970s have also exerted pressure to change. On the one hand they have enabled manufacturers to offer ever more sophisticated products. For instance, it is now possible for microprocessors to monitor fuel consumption and the wear of individual parts, to improve safety and comfort, and to read road signs. On the other hand, technological advances in manufacturing methods ensure a steady flow on to the market of more sophisticated production methods, such as industrial robots, 'in search of applications'. Such pressures forced manufacturers to be constantly on the look-out for methods which are cheaper, more efficient and produce higher quality goods and they could not afford to slip behind their competitors in making use of them.

Since the late 1960s car manufacturers have encountered pressure to review production methods from another source, namely from their employees and from the trade unions who represent them. Growing concern with the quality of working life and the desire for increased participation in the work process has led to demands for working environments which are safer, healthier and more pleasant, and for jobs which are at the same time less arduous and repetitive, and more skilled and more intellectually rewarding.

There is wide diversity in the seriousness with which different manufacturers viewed this pressure. In Sweden, for instance, Saab and Volvo took it very seriously. They saw that social changes, particularly in education and upbringing, had fuelled changes in people's expectations so that they would no longer work wholeheartedly on traditional assembly lines. The fragmentation of jobs and the tyranny of work tied to the pace of machines were out of keeping with people's growing desire for work in which they could use their skills and take some pride. Although some 30 per cent of production workers in the car industry in Sweden were actually Finns together with a sprinkling of Yugoslavs, Saab and Volvo did not feel that labour discontent could be averted by relying on such peoples' lack of industrial sophistication and their gratitude at finding relatively well-paid employment. Nor did these companies feel there was sufficient long-term advantage in shifting production to comparatively under-developed parts of the world, like Brazil and Korea, where people's expectations were not so high. Saab and Volvo decided that the only viable way of easing problems of discontent arising from the nature of the work was to change the nature of the work.

General Motors, Renault, Fiat and the German manufacturers took a broadly similar view, although they did not all feel the problem to be as immediate or as serious as did the Swedes, for several reasons. They did not share the labour shortages encountered in Sweden in the late 1960s and early 1970s. Their education systems had not created such highly qualified production workers as was the case in Sweden. Car manufacturers outside Sweden also felt that the migrant workers whom to greater or lesser extent they all employed (largely from Southern Europe or, in the case of Renault, from North Africa) would provide a satisfactory source of labour to suppplement nationals for some time to come. In addition, the Scandinavians, with their longer experience of industrial democracy, tend to take the quality of working life rather more seriously.

By contrast, British Leyland did not share this anlaysis. The industrial relations turbulence they encountered in the late 1960s was, in the view of senior management, largely the result of a decayed piece-work system, rather than of a change in employees' expectations. Certainly the piece-work system was causing problems, but what was behind those problems? Many would contend that people's determination to control the piece-work system was at least in part an attempt to re-assert some of the influence over matters affecting them which had largely been lost to those in conventional line jobs. But because the changing expectations of employees were not seen as important by British Leyland, the changes in work organization which did take place, notably in the new Metro facility, were dictated largely by the considerations of production engineering.

Whatever their view of the importance of changes in employees' expectations, all the manufacturers responded to the pressure for change which they were encountering by seeking new production methods which would be adaptable and flexible. Conventional assembly lines were not sufficiently responsive. Not only do they lack flexibility in a technical sense, they also encourage inflexible attitudes amongst both managers and production workers – and this in itself works against adaptability. They do not equip manufacturers to keep pace with what is going on in the outside world.

The fact that business reasons such as these have provided the impetus for change has proved to be important. It has meant that when obstacles have arisen – as in all cases they have – manufacturers have tried to find ways round the obstacles, rather than abandon attempts to proceed.

This is not always the case when organizations embark on such changes. Suppose, for instance, that the main impetus comes from the Personnel Department – where perhaps some undefined idea has arisen that the Company should treat its people more like adults, or that it should not drop behind other companies in the application of fashionable ideas – then the new approach is likely to be abandoned as soon as the first obstacle is encountered. A clearly identified business reason for the attempt is an essential requirement for success.

But while all the manufacturers had sound commercial considerations in mind, most of them were also quite clear that they must not attempt such changes at the expense of their employees. In the words of a Volvo spokesman, 'in business today you cannot separate economic goals from social goals. What is done for commercial reasons and what is done for human reasons must be mutually supportive.'[1] This kind of thinking is behind Renault's 'profiling method', which enables the company, including its foremen and development engineers, to compare different options for structuring work from the point of view of those who would be doing the jobs.

3. The changes made

In deciding what particular changes to make the companies were influenced by several interrelated factors:

(i) The type of car they produce. For example, Volkswagen took the view that they could not imitate the methods used by Volvo when they were producing some 5,000 cars per day, the cheapest costing only DM 5,600, compared with Volvo's production of substantially fewer cars per day, the cheapest of which costs about three times as much as the cheapest VW. (However, it does not follow that such radical methods are necessarily inappropriate to high volume production.)

(ii) How seriously they viewed their predicament. This also influenced the extent to which manufacturers were prepared to be radical. For instance, although labour turnover and absenteeism were generally felt to be higher than acceptable, the rates varied considerably. In Sweden they were particularly high. Labour turnover was often up to 50 per cent nationally in manufacturing (and higher in parts of Saab and Volvo during the late 1960s). Absenteeism had reached over 15 per cent nationally by 1976, partly at least because of the comparative liberality of the Swedish social security system. In addition, absenteeism and labour turnover were intensified by problems of labour shortage not encountered elsewhere.

(iii) The home country's experience of similar change processes. Although manufacturers of cars are strongly influenced by the need to keep pace with what their competitors abroad are doing, they are also affected by the activities of manufacturers of other goods in their own country. Thus in Sweden, where the use of socio-technical analysis was relatively widespread, Saab and Volvo were talking in terms of the need to adapt technology to people. In other countries, such as Italy, where such an approach was not so familiar, Fiat was less radical, talking of finding the best compromise between technological requirements and the expectations of their employees.

(iv) Their priorities. Within the overall aim of increasing profitability each manufacturer identified particular priorities of his own. For instance, General Motors in the USA felt that such a massive corporation needed to increase its ability to cope with the unpredictability of the future. Therefore they chose to begin by actively involving employees in a comprehensive process of organization development, with the aim of increasing flexibility by changing attitudes.

British Leyland in the UK also gave priority to involving employees, but for quite different reasons, springing from an urgent need to reduce the turbulence of industrial relations, as well as a need to respond to anticipated legislation following the Bullock Report. These pressures resulted in an Employee Participation Scheme which incidentally enabled matters like the organization of work and the planning of new facilities to be discussed outside traditional arrangements for negotiating.

Saab, Volvo, Fiat, Renault and German manufacturers like Opel, Audi, Volkswagen, BMW and Daimler Benz concentrated on using new technology and new production methods to improve the nature of jobs and the environment at work, the Germans taking a largely ergonomic and engineering approach, often using funds made available by the German Government's Humanization of Work Programme.

So there were differences in approach. Indeed, in the early 1970s manufacturers were stressing the individuality of their approach and expressing doubts about what they saw their competitors as attempting. Despite such differences there was a good deal of common ground, both in terms of the overall framework in which the companies saw the project and in the terms of the changes themselves. All saw themselves embarking on a long-term project which, initially at least, would be experimental in the sense of trying to learn as much as possible for application both in existing plants and in the design of new ones.

Because the aim was to learn – and to do so within the context of economic competition – the results were carefully evaluated. This evaluation itself required a new approach, combining the analysis of hard data with the careful use of judgement where hard data was either not available or was inappropriate. Also, because the aim was to learn, none of the manufacturers used a standard package of change or any fixed technique. Instead they were totally pragmatic, doing what they felt best suited their own particular circumstances. Yet the changes were not made piecemeal: each saw his own effort as a planned attempt to stay profitable in unpredictable and rapidly changing circumstances.

Whatever their starting point and their priorities, most manufacturers saw that the work they were undertaking could potentially affect all aspects of their operation: job content, work organization, technology, the involvement of trade unions and employees, payment system, working conditions, and even the company's position in the community. The major changes made fall into two interrelated categories: technology and work organization. These changes were reinforced by others in training, in payment systems, and in the social aspects of employment policy.

Changes in technology

The fundamental aim behind all the changes made was to increase the flexibility and efficiency of methods of production. Advances in technology enabled manufacturers to do this. Such advances also enabled them to achieve another of their aims: that of improving the working environment, making it more safe, more healthy and more pleasant; in conjunction with this they hoped to be able to reduce conflict in industrial relations which was greatest in some of the most unpleasant jobs, notably in welding. For instance, in the painting process new materials like non-liquid paints and epoxy powders, new processes like electro-phoresis, and specially designed application cabins offered several advantages. It became possible to take men out of the unpleasant and unhealthy paint process. Not only did this improve health and safety, it also gave the flexibility needed to offer customers a wide colour range, as well as improving efficiency and quality. However skilled a man becomes at paint-spraying, he is still far more likely to waste paint and to spray unevenly than is an automatic machine.

Welding is another process that has been transformed. Previously, men working singly but on a line applied each weld separately. This system which was unpleasant, tedious and too often inaccurate, has been largely replaced by automated multiweld systems which enable huge numbers of welds, often one hundred or more at a time, to be completed in a single, safe, fast and highly accurate operation.

Multi-headed machine tools, or transfers, complete a whole range of tasks required to machine such sub-assembly pieces as an engine block or head. Thus milling, turning, boring, broaching and so on can all be carried out accurately and very quickly. Pneumatic 'iron hands' in press shops now remove completed pressings from the presses, far more quickly and safely than could be done under the old, onerous manual system. More recently developed systems now enable the sheet metal to be carried automatically along a line of up to seven presses, freeing men from the whole of the tedious and potentially dangerous process.

The use of improved materials facilitates such developments. New, thinner, double-deep drawing steels are more easy to manipulate and help to achieve stronger, lighter structures. Advances in plastics and injection moulding and in aluminium enable manufacturers to use these lighter materials more widely, thus simplifying parts of the assembly process and resulting in lighter, and therefore more economical, vehicles.

These developments have taken place gradually. More revolutionary has been the introduction of robots. For some time industrial robots have been bringing speed and accuracy to the burdensome tasks of loading, stacking and carrying and to the unpleasant tasks of surface coating and welding. Recently there have been great advances. A survey carried out in 1982 in West Germany,[2] for instance, found industrial robots to be the most significant form of new technology in use in that country. Most of them are to be found in motor manufacturing where they are most important in 'body in white' and paint shops. They are also used in a wide range of production procedures, such as the positioning of crankshafts in cases, inserting rear axles into welding machines, and applying underseal.

On the technical side the greatest scope for inproving flexibility, efficiency and quality is offered by the even more recent development of fully automatic, computer-controlled production systems. It is in such systems that the most significant developments of the foreseeable future are likely to take place. They offer the great advantage of reducing the cost of work in progress, which can contribute significantly to making manufacturing more economic.

An example of a highly efficient application of such a system is the 'body in white' facility for British Leyland's Metro. This is how some of these new systems work in practice. The Metro body shell consists of some 85 components brought together into 26 major sub-assemblies by resistance spot-welding and fusion welding. The sub-assembly facility uses multi-welders, automatic transfers, turn-over services and solid-state controlled welding equipment. All major machines are provided with automatic diagnostic equipment.

Components arrive from the automated warehouse in pallets and are deposited in queuing tables providing an in-process buffer store between the warehouse and the sub-assembly facility. Single, dedicated multi-welders produce simple sub-assemblies (vehicle doors, tail-gate and front fenders), operating on a cycle time of 25 seconds. The more complex sub-assemblies (side panels, front end under-frame, main floor and underframe floor assembly) require duplicate facilities and operate on a cycle time of 50 seconds.

A mini-computer controls and governs the sequence of manufacturing movements and operations. Mimic panels show the exact position of the machine in the cycle and automatic diagnosis is provided. Visual Display Units (VDUs) summarize all the diagnostic information. Completed components are automatically transferred to conveyor systems for delivery to body-framing stations. The loading of machines and certain welding operations are the only tasks which are performed manually.

Renault too are using computerized production management to enable them to cope with the wide range of variants in tyres, colours and optional extras that customers now require. At their plants at Flins and Douai, for example, the supply of components, the management of their progress to assembly and the control of stock are controlled in this way. A more advanced degree of computerized production management is used in a flexible workshop set up by Renault Véhicules at Bouthéon, where a computer controls the movements of several types of part between the various machine-tools which bring them to a finished state.

Systems of this kind require the car itself and the production process to be designed together; the one has to be devised for the other, not merely adapted to it. This calls for modular systems which simplify assembly and make it possible to cope with the wide variety of alternative versions which manufacturers increasingly need to offer. For instance, the VW Golf in 1982 offered 4 different roofs, 18 different car fronts, 2 side parts each for left and right, 3 different front floors and 4 different rear floors. For the body alone this makes a total of 3,000 theoretical bodywork alternatives. To make optimum use of the welding transfer line, the differences in the various versions are, as far as possible, taken into account in the production of the sub-assemblies.

To achieve a higher level of automation in assembly too and to move away from the conventional long line, an attempt is being made to change the structure of the product to enable as many sub-assemblies as possible to be fully assembled and tested, so that final assembly can consist simply of fitting together these highly-integrated sub-assemblies. In individual pre-assembly systems this allows both a considerably greater degree of automation and, in manual work, ergonomically better job structuring. It also offers scope to restructure work, lengthen the job cycle time of individuals and increase job satisfaction.

Fiat has made great advances in the automation of the production process and the concomitant design of a product with this in mind. In fact over the period 1971–80 about 50 per cent of all direct manual workers in Fiat's car factories became affected by new measures, involving what in some cases are quite radical changes in technology and the means of production. The three main aspects of this process are an increase in the level of automation; a gradual move towards flexible automation; and a change from the concept of the 'automatic machine' towards that of the 'automatic production system'.

The table summarizes what has been happening.

Progress in bodywork assembly at FIAT Auto between 1961 and 1980

Year	Innovation	Model	Remarks
1961	automatic welding for entire car floor	1300–1600	similar assembly systems were only adopted by other car manufacturers in 1965
1966	complete pre-assembly of the chassis (sides and roof) in multiple welding machines on transfer lines	124–127 128	a reduction of manual effort; lack of flexibility; the plant can only be used for the model for which it was designed
1972	automatic equipment for welding not just tacking the body	127	closer tolerances; further reduction of heavy work
1973	16 robots employed in the final welding operations	132	greater flexibility; more space and light around the machines
1974	completely automated assembly of the floor, sides, roof and chassis	131	
1975	Digitron automatic plant for bolting the engine to the vehicle body; automatic spraying of sound-deadening material	131	further reduction in heavy work; lack of flexibility
1977	paint undercoat sprayed on as a powder by robots	126	energy saving; cleaner, safer environment; flexibility
1978	Robogate: completely automated, robotized welding of bodywork components. Robotized, mechanized enamelling of the body exterior	Ritmo (Strada) 126–128	completely flexible
1980	LAM: asynchronous engine assembly line	various models	highly flexible

Digitron, introduced in 1975, Robogate, introduced in 1978, and LAM, introduced in 1980, are examples of highly flexible 'sub-systems' which have been achieved by re-planning whole areas of the car assembly cycle. Because they are such important innovations they are described briefly below.

The **Digitron** system represents a first step towards replacing the assembly line with a series of interdependent 'production modules'. This process will be advanced further by structural changes in the product (a different electrical system in cars, for instance), and by changes in a number of other stages of the production process (e.g. painting and welding). The system is concerned with the most critical point of the assembly cycle: the marriage of the two major components – the body and the power train. It is here that maximum flexibility is required in order to match successfully all the different options of engine and body that the market demands.

The heart of Digitron is the computerized production control system, the influence of which is felt throughout the entire working cycle. It guarantees greater production flexibility so that changes in demand can be coped with more easily and greater flexibility in the use of manpower, as well as improving quality control by giving warnings if the bolting-up stations are not functioning properly or to the right torque. It also improves production control by identifying any bottlenecks.

Linked with the computerized production system are automatic handling trolleys, or Robocarriers. These have made it possible to do away with the line because they combine all the advantages of pre-dictability with the additional advantage of being far more flexible than any conventional system. Controlled by the various production crews, they allow work in progress to accumulate, they can be re-routed to cope with abnormal situations as they arise, and they allow many operations to be carried out at fixed stations without inter-rupting the production cycle.

Digitron's automatic store also enhances flexibility by acting as a buffer, absorbing irregularities in the flow of parts between prepara-tion and fixing points.

Time control is flexible too. Maximum times for carrying out different operations have been arrived at by bargaining between man-agement and unions and the production teams have discretion within these limits. Thus preparation and job times are no longer directly tied to the speed of the line. The Robocarrier moves from one station to the next as ordered by the crew; operations like screwing up bolts, which used to require people to work in uncomfortable positions, have been eliminated. At some points team working offers people more discretion and independence. Noise has been reduced and the abolition of overhead conveyors has increased light and the feeling of space.

The **Robogate** is another highly automated system, involving only very few people in preparing parts, carrying out maintenance and taking corrective action when something goes wrong. As with Digitron, the heart of the Robogate system is a complex automated information system which controls all aspects of the production process. Linked with this information system are:

the Robocarrier: an electrical transporter controlled by a central computer. Driven by electric accumulators, the Robocarrier is guided by an electromagnetic field generated by radio-frequency currents channelled through a cable sunk in the floor;

the pallets: the supports on which the body shell is held firmly in position throughout the welding cycle;

the robot: a programmed, multi-purpose, flexible machine. There are between 2 and 5 robots at each welding station and they are usually larger than the component to be welded.

The Robogate system provides several advantages:

flexibility: when appropriately tooled the system allows 4 different models to be produced on the same plant without interrupting production;

an improvement in environmental conditions: as well as reducing the arduous aspects of the job, the Robogate's flexibility offers operators more discretion about how their work is organized. The compact structure of the welding stations allows more space and light, and noise is reduced;

a reduction in investment costs: because costs can be spread over the 2, 3 or 4 models which can be produced by the plant.

LAM (Asynchronous Assembly Line) is an innovation in engine assembly guided by the same philosophy as the Robogate and Digitron. Again the essential features are automation and computerization which determine and control the flow of production. Thus it has been possible to replace the traditional line system conventionally used for assembling engines with a series of assembly 'islands', each responsible for a particular module in the production process. Between the islands are buffer stores, with a storage capacity of up to 50 minutes. These intermediate stores give LAM operators freedom to arrange their own working and rest time individually, without any ill effects on the regular flow or total volume of production.

Linking the system are 'sliding lines' of robotized trolleys moving at ground level, similar to the Robocarriers but smaller. Each can carry two engines simultaneously. They are equipped with a pallet-lifting device and are used to move store racks and to load and unload engines automatically on to and from the benches at the work station. When an operator has completed his task he presses a button to inform the central computer system; trolleys then remove the finished item and deliver a new one.

The trolleys' movements are controlled by a computerized information system which directs all the automatic stores and the flow of parts both to and from the buffer stores and to and from the individual work stations. Thus, as it moves from one work group to another, each assembly is supplied, both automatically and manually, with all the necessary parts for the next stage.

This information system can programme the production of the various components needed, as well as plan the most efficient use of the trolleys and the optimum levels of stocks to be held in the automated stores.

The LAM system thus offers the following advantages:

it enhances flexibility: the system of computerized management allows about 100 different types of engine to be produced;

quality control improves: if an operator realizes that he has made a mistake, or if there are problems in assembly, the engine can be diverted to a special section where the fault can be rectified; also the automated transfers embody automatic checks on quality control and the causes of any breakdowns are notified directly to the central information system – thus the chargehand has a complete picture of any problems and can tell operators what mistakes are being made and suggest ways of avoiding them;

better working conditions: uncomfortable 'raised arm' operations are eliminated; working space has been increased; stores and racks become more functional; environmental pollution has decreased; and noise is reduced; individual job cycle times are also considerably increased, allowing scope for more discretion and for more satisfying jobs to be created.

These examples demonstrate how manufacturers used technological advances to solve some challenging technical problems. The central problem in moving away from traditional assembly lines lay in the fact that the speed of the line conventionally determines the entire nature of the production process. Work comes along the line to the worker at predetermined intervals, the worker completes his task in the predetermined time and the piece continues along the line.

It is precisely this machine pacing that has been found to be unsatisfactory to manufacturers and their employees alike – and ultimately even to the customers. To the manufacturer it brings inflexibility in production and balance problems which are also time consuming because changes in production requirements cause problems of rebalancing the timing of work with line speed and operator numbers. Malfunctions in one spot affect the whole line because faulty work moves inexorably along the line, without much opportunity for correction until the end. This leads to faulty products and dissatisfied customers. For the employee it creates fragmented, low-skilled and stressful jobs.

The advantage of the new forms of technology and work organization is that the 'drive' or control is supplied not by technology, but by people. Flexibility is thus increased; quality control is more immediate and more effective; and balance loss problems are diminished because, aided by special carriers which they control and by flexible buffer stocks, the people involved can sort them out themselves quite straightforwardly as they work. The problem was how to devise efficient production systems without the customary regulating role which had been supplied by machine pacing. In surmounting this problem technical changes were vital. Without them far less would have been possible. But they are only part of the story, as the examples given above have begun to show. Other complementary changes in work organization were also required, both to help exploit the potential advantages offered by the new forms of technology, and to increase operational flexibility and the job satisfaction of the operator when constraints of space, time and money delayed or prevented technical improvements. Such joint design of technical systems and forms of work organization could be called using the socio-technical approach. But this was certainly not a term used by manufacturers, who saw themselves only as trying to solve operational problems, rather than applying behavioural science techniques.

Changes in work organization

The extent of changes in the way work is organized varies greatly both among manufacturers and among their various plants. The most radical changes have been made in Sweden, in the new Saab and Volvo plants, where the design of new technology and new forms of work organization have gone hand in hand to an extent not apparent elsewhere. The result has been that employees, working as a team in fixed off-line assembly areas, are able to build complete items like engines, gear boxes and other sub-assemblies. The workers themselves decide who will carry out which tasks, depending on skill, experience and personal preference. New mechanized or automated transport systems, using, for instance, tracked or air-cushioned conveyors, were specially designed to bring parts to the operators and to take away completed work. The operator was not controlled by the speed of these systems. Reserve, or 'buffer' stocks of parts were incorporated to increase operators' flexibility and the extent to which they could control the speed and method of their work.

Light, self-adjusting machines capable of carrying out a number of operations were introduced. Parts within off-line assembly areas were moved by special hoisting gear and tracked carts. At Volvo's Kalmar plant the piece being assembled – the body, or after the marriage with the gear box, the whole car – was placed on a platform which could be tilted through ninety degrees to make all parts of the workpiece easily accessible. These assembly platforms also formed part of the computer-controlled transport system. Physical effort was thereby cut to a minimum and it was often possible for women to do work which previously required the strength of a man, thus increasing production flexibility.

The provision of a transport system controlled by the operator, combined with buffer stocks before and after each working group to store incoming and outgoing work, offered the teams and their company much increased flexibility. By arrangement amongst themselves they can vary their work rate within overall production requirements, building up stocks of completed work to enable them to cope with disruptions, or to accumulate extra time for breaks, or work at a slower pace for a period if they wish. The scope for offering choice to people in these groups was great and the potential for increasing job satisfaction and commitment relatively high.

Satisfied though Saab and Volvo are with the results of these innovations they have not introduced them into all their plants because constraints and local needs vary. Kalmar, for instance, was a new plant, specially designed to suit a product, a technical system and a social system designed jointly. Such scope to innovate is not offered in existing plants with conventional lines, although even there much can be achieved by using such aids as buffer stores.

Other manufacturers have not felt it appropriate to be as innovative as Saab and Volvo. Indeed there has arisen what is sometimes called the 'Kalmar' syndrome, a tendency on the part of other manufacturers and various academics to reject Kalmar as a 'failure', although the evidence (described below under 'What happened as a result') demonstrates that by every criterion it is a success. However, despite differences of view and approach, the manufacturers all aimed, in various ways and to varying extents, to reduce machine pacing and the fragmentation of jobs associated with conventional lines. Here are some typical examples of what has been achieved which illustrate less radical applications of some of the ideas used at Kalmar.

(i) Job cycle times have been increased.
It is hard to offer people work in which they can take pride if the task they do takes only a very short time to complete. Jobs with a short cycle become, almost by definition, routine and monotonous and lacking in scope to use discretion. Some people like such jobs, but most do not. Therefore all manufacturers have made efforts to increase cycle times. Most scope to do this is offered when work is taken off lines and completed on fixed stations, either by groups or individuals. By using such methods Saab, for instance, estimate that their cycle times have increased from 1.8 minutes to 30 minutes and, while many jobs at Volvo take around 30 minutes, they also report cycle times of up to 4 hours and even longer in parts of their truck division.

Even when the work continues to be done on assembly lines, dramatic increases in cycle times have been achieved. For instance, BMW report increases of between 10 and 20 times. The introduction of enriched individual jobs into the assembly of radiators at Audi increased cycle times from between 5.9 and 7.8 minutes to as much as 25 minutes. And at Fiat's Mirafiori plant some checking and testing operations have been restructured to convert jobs lasting about one minute into jobs lasting 19 minutes.

(ii) Job content has been improved.
Such increases in cycle times permit the rebuilding of fragmented jobs,

for instance by using job rotation, enlargement and enrichment. Thus people were offered greater variety, more responsibility and more opportunity to develop their skills.

Group working was one method widely adopted for rebuilding fragmented jobs. It was successfully used in conjunction with off-line working at Saab and Volvo but it was also used to improve the situation where lines were retained. For instance, individual jobs tied to a line can be linked both to each other and to separate off-line jobs which share something in common with them, like maintenance or quality control. This kind of group working encourages the increase of technical skills through doing a wider range of tasks. And, just as important, it offers the interest and challenge of working with other people which, in itself, gives the opportunity for a new range of interpersonal skills to develop.

But group working is not the only way of improving job content. Another method often used was to build up, or enrich, individual jobs – off-line, prior to the line, or parallel with it. This created jobs which offered people more scope and by combining this enrichment with the use of buffer stocks the jobs became more independent of line tempo. This idea has been used with success in Germany, for instance, at Opel. Originally, on the cellulosing line an inspector checked and noted any polishing defects. A polisher then corrected the defect and the work went back to the inspector for a re-check. Now polishers do the whole job themselves, being completely responsible for polishing, looking for defects, correcting them and reinspecting for an unblemished finish.

Another widely used innovation was to allow workers to move along the line carrying out several stages of assembly instead of just one. Thus some of the early work at Renault enlarged a line job from one to twenty-two different operations. The approach is also common in Britain. It is a useful way of lessening the adverse effects of machine pacing and short cycles and can be relatively easily implemented on conventional lines.

In many cases use of this idea has been facilitated by replacing one long line with several slower-moving, parallel, shorter lines, a technique offering several options which Fiat, for example, have developed with great success. At their Cassino plant, which was specially built for this purpose, they installed four short parallel lines instead of one long conventional line to carry out trim and final assembly on the Fiat 126. By moving along the line with the work-piece, workers were able to carry out all the tasks on one sub-assembly. The job cycles offered were three or four times greater than they would have been on a conventional line and the system offered not only greater production flexibility but was less vulnerable to the effects of disruptions and to balancing problems. Such lines have become known as 'Cassino lines'.

Fiat developed the idea a stage further in their Mirafiori plant in Turin where they use it in assembling engines. There, four short lines, each broken twice by buffer stocks, replace the conventional long line. At each break in the line there is the facility of transferring the sub-assembly to an adjacent line if necessary. Thus flexibility, and the scope for operators to choose and to enrich jobs, is greatly enhanced. BMW use a similar idea rather differently at their new Dingolfing plant. Here three short parallel lines broken into sections by buffer stocks provided an opportunity for group work on enlarged tasks. The buffers also allowed individuals and groups to vary their rhythms.

(iii) More choice has been offered to employees.

The smooth running of the conventional assembly line depends on uniformity. Thus people are typically offered little or no choice about what they do or how they do it. The newer methods aimed to increase the extent of people's discretion in a variety of ways:

altering line speed – this includes the possibilities of stopping, slowing or accelerating the line by joint decision, or even by individual decision where appropriate;

varying work rhythm – the use of buffer stocks between individuals or groups has been widespread and successful;

choice about where and how to work – for instance, in a Daimler Benz transmission plant people can choose between working on long or short lines, working individually or in groups, and assembling sub-parts or the whole of an item like a bus gear box;

choice about who does what – choice of this kind fits in well with the off-line group working typical of new Swedish plants like Volvo's Kalmar;

choice about working hours – this kind of choice is most common in Sweden where freedom from the line is greatest and where in some plants workers who have completed their production quota can go home; by varying their work pace they can finish whenever it suits them (it is possible that choice about working hours may soon be taken further in Sweden so that each person's contracted hours will be tailored to their individual needs, giving employees more scope to arrange their lives as they wish; it would also, it is hoped, both reduce absenteeism and make its levels more predictable for the employer);

choice about who will work – some of the early work at Volvo offered choice of a rather different kind: for instance, in one upholstery shop women could choose whether to cover a single work station themselves or in conjunction with one or more women, with whom they might also co-operate over care of each other's children.

(iv) Employees have been consulted more.

Technology influences attitudes and habits of mind. Thus workers tied to machine-paced jobs are not traditionally regarded by their managers, perhaps not even by themselves, as a fruitful source of ideas. So they are seldom consulted. This can intensify any feeling they have of being adjuncts to the line which, in turn, can further sap their initiative and ability to contribute. Manufacturers felt they had to reverse this because they needed their employees' ideas to improve the company's performance. To an extent this happened naturally. As people became accustomed to doing more responsible, more thought-provoking work their imaginations were stimulated. This provided companies with a reservoir of suggestions which they could use in improving company performance still further.

Most manufacturers tried to find ways of channelling these ideas to ensure that they were not wasted. For instance, Saab set up 'production' groups to involve people in identifying and solving everyday operational problems and 'development' groups to involve them in developing new methods, new technology and new plant designs. Other companies used similar methods more informally, without giving the groups specific names.

There were also cases where the main thrust of the company's programme – even more important than improving jobs – was to involve people more in order to engage their efforts in improving the company's performance. General Motors is the most prominent example. All factory managers at General Motors are required to include an item on the 'quality of working life' in their annual reports. Beyond this, worker participation was encouraged in several optional but nevertheless consistent ways, the options on offer ranging from the wider use of group working to the introduction of 'quality circles', an idea adopted from Japan, where it has been used with great success. Basically it entails groups of workers who volunteer to meet regularly to discuss and resolve common problems – again an idea which has been used elsewhere, for instance at Volvo, without giving it name or formality.

Other changes

These major changes in work organization and technology were reinforced by parallel changes in training, in payment systems and in the social aspects of employment policy.

(i) `Training

There was heavy emphasis on training, not just for operators, but also for supervisors, managers and for members of the various committees set up to see projects through. Operators needed new technical skills to do enriched jobs well. Supervisors and managers needed new technical skills too, but it was even more important for them to learn the best way of giving support to people taking on more responsible and independent jobs.

Where autonomous groups were introduced, and where committees were set up, team building and communication skills became a vital element of training.

Preparing people for the changes was another priority. General Motors, for instance, in conjunction with the American United Auto Workers Union (UAW) carried out company-wide programmes focusing on changing attitudes and giving more information about the enterprise. In Germany, Opel prepared the ground by training 5 per cent of the workforce to act as leaders in introducing new work structure. They also trained 332 others (more than half of them migrant workers) to act as trainers.

(ii) Payment systems

The lack of suitable payment systems acted as a considerable constraint on progress. British Leyland, for instance, found that their traditional piece-work system was not sufficiently flexible. All changes in work rate or job content had to be separately negotiated and with more than 250 bargaining units, negotiations were endless. This was an important reason for their attempt to introduce a participation scheme which would enable work organization to be discussed outside the traditional negotiating mode.

Wage systems based on job evaluation, on the other hand, provided a good framework, especially where they were jointly administered by management and the trade unions and where bargaining was based on single units. The Scandinavian and German manufacturers were long familiar with such systems and where such systems were not already in use companies tended to introduce them, as they did in Italy in the early 1970s. People taking on work demanding higher skills could then be given an appropriate increase in pay. Where assembly was carried out by autonomous groups, as at Saab and Volvo, premium systems with a group incentive element were introduced.

(iii) The social aspects of employment policy

Most manufacturers also improved the social aspects of their employment policy, which was particularly helpful where State provisions were not well developed. The changes made varied in lavishness and kind, but common elements were:

greatly improved sports and social facilities;

greater attention to the health of employees, involving, for instance, new medical centres, research into occupational diseases and preventive health care;

help with housing problems, especially for immigrants;

opportunities for education and training within working hours as well as outside – a special feature being language training for immigrants.

Obviously many of these schemes offered advantages to the companies, as well as to their employees. It is, for instance, preferable to employ healthy people who can speak the local language than people constantly on sick leave with whom communication is difficult. Since some of the schemes involved extensive work with local communities and local authorities, the company was able to improve its local image. However, manufacturers have stated that these ventures also have a social, as well as an economic side. They feel that they are an important aspect of their responsibility as employers, worthwhile doing on their merits and not just for possible economic gain.

4. How the changes were made

As many organizations have found, people tend to feel threatened by change and, when they do, they resist it, even though the proposed changes are intended to help them. People who resist change will not try to make it work and the benefit to the company of introducing it will be restricted, no matter how advanced the new technology and no matter how ingenious the innovations in work organization.

In order to prevent this danger from bedevilling their efforts each manufacturer carefully explained what was planned and many, as we have seen, introduced special training to help people adapt. Some were prepared to go further. They felt that while information and training were vital they could not be the whole answer because people need a stake in something if they are to be fully committed to making it work. And having a stake in something comes not so much from knowing all about it as from having helped to create it. But involving people in planning a new system has another benefit. No matter how good a company's design engineers, it is hard for them to envisage all the effects of working in the new way. People directly engaged on production are in many ways the best source of ideas about this. It was therefore sensible to encourage them to make their contribution.

The problem was how best to achieve this in huge companies working all the time under the pressure of keeping production going. The chief way of involving workers was inevitably through their trade unions. Given the long history of trade unionism in the industry and the high percentage of membership this was the obvious, natural and appropriate channel. Moreover, any failure adequately to consult trade union officials would have left them feeling threatened by the prospect of change. Then they would have behaved like anybody else under threat: they would have resisted what threatened them. While this background was common to all companies, the exact form and extent of trade union involvement varied.

In Sweden, for instance, industrial relations had been relatively stable for many years. Managers and trade union representatives had come to trust each other and respect each other's motives even when they differed and this gave a good background for the new ventures. Conflicts did arise during discussions, as was inevitable when managers and trade unionists alike were embarking on a radical new process, but differences tended to be settled constructively. This was achieved because well-informed, trained, experienced managers and trade union representatives worked within well-established and respected procedures.

The mutual understanding that made their success possible had only arisen gradually and as the result of hard work on both sides. When, some years before, the process of co-determination was introduced, both managers and trade union representatives had difficulties in adjusting. It did not always prove easy to give up existing prerogatives and take the risk of working together in a different way. However, by the time Saab and Volvo began their projects the problem had largely been overcome. The challenge was not so much in working together with the trade unions as in tackling the technical and social problems of the particular projects. The situation in Germany was similar.

But this was not the case with the other manufacturers. All shared with the Swedes the technical and social problems, but elsewhere managers and trade union representatives were trying to tackle them without the same solid background of co-determination and nowhere did they involve the trade unions as fully as did the Swedes.

At British Leyland in the UK, for example, the relationship between management and trade unions was one of adversaries, in the traditional collective bargaining sense. The only normal mode of discussion was negotiation. By the mid-1970s the company had resolved to introduce an Employee Participation Scheme, partly in an attempt to alleviate its industrial relations problems and partly in response to ideas about industrial democracy fuelled by the possibility of legislation following the Bullock Report. One spin-off of this scheme was that it provided a suitable framework within which to discuss changes in work organization with the trade unions. The result was that consultations about the new Metro facility were extensive and constructive, though to achieve this success both sides had to give up existing prerogatives. Management, for instance, shared more information with the unions than ever before and invited union comments before taking decisions. The trade unions gave up the right to negotiate the rate of work, negotiating only the criteria on which work rates would be established. They also relaxed existing demarcation lines – an important concession in the UK where the number of unions involved is relatively high compared with most other counties.

But it takes a long time for such a process of joint consultation to become securely established. After several years of useful, but by no means smooth, experience on the Metro facility many of the problems of working together remain unsolved, as the suspension of the Employee Participation Scheme demonstrates.

In the USA the basic problems were similar, but the context was different. Management had been introducing new ideas like job enrichment since the late 1950s, but they had not consulted employees much about their implementation. By the mid-1960s when General Motors launched their organization development programme the prevailing climate, especially in the big corporations, was still one in which managers stressed their right to manage. The trade unions were regarded more as adversaries in negotiation than as partners. Thus General Motors' decision to embark on the organization development project with the involvement of the trade unions was a new departure. For it to stand a chance of success managers had to let the unions, as well as employees, have a voice in Company decisions as never before.

The large American trade unions, for their part, tended to reject ideas like organization development, or at least to be highly sceptical of them. Overall their attitude was one of suspicion. They saw their role in traditional terms: that of improving pay and working conditions by tough negotiations rather than by any form of co-operation with management.

They are becoming more flexible now. But in the mid-1960s the UAW was almost the only large union willing to risk the kind of joint venture proposed by General Motors. It took the risk because it saw the chance of increasing the influence of the union and its members over company decisions.

To safeguard their traditional interests while taking this risk the UAW made its co-operation dependent on three conditions:

(i)   the work rate was not to be pushed up by the programme;

(ii) the programme would not cause lay-offs;

(iii) wages, welfare payments and general working conditions would be negotiated subsequently.

Management's agreement to those conditions demonstrated their own willingness to take risks and be flexible about relinquishing existing prerogatives and so a gradual change of attitude began on both sides.

In France and Italy there were similar problems in bringing about changes in attitude, but they were made even more difficult to handle by the way the trade unions were organized. Whereas in most countries people tend to join the union which represents their craft or industry, in France and Italy they tend to join the union that represents their politics. The largest and most influential unions in France (the CGT) and in Italy (the CGIL) are essentially Communist. This determined their attitude to company initiatives at Renault and Fiat.

The CGT was keen that the programme at Renault should go ahead because they could see their members' jobs and working conditions improving as a result. Accordingly they were consulted by management and they put forward their own ideas. At the same time they believed that changes in the way work was organized could never truly benefit workers within the political framework of capitalism. Thus they could never work jointly with managers as could the Swedish, or even American unions. It remains to be seen how far political changes in France will influence their attitude.

In Italy the three major unions CGIL, CISL and UIL were united in seeing changes in work organization as a potentially important means of increasing workers' control – initially over day-to-day decisions within the plants, but ultimately over national political decisions. These were not objectives shared by management. Such views posed practical problems which Renault and Fiat managers had to solve if they were to secure the necessary dialogue with the trade unions. In both countries a *modus vivendi* was reached, enabling consultation to go ahead without the principles of either side being compromised.

Manufacturers in Sweden, Germany, France and Italy also had to consider how best to involve the works councils as well as the trade unions. In Sweden and Germany this was a familiar and accepted procedure. For instance, when work on the new Volvo projects began around 1970 the company already had about twenty years' experience of participation within the works councils. In France and Italy on the other hand works councils were still relatively embryonic. At Fiat, for example, the legal establishment of works councils, a result of the industrial and political disturbances of the 'long, hot autumn' of 1969, more or less coincided with the start of the Company's work reorganization projects. This meant that the involvement of inexperienced employee representatives with managers who were also inexperienced was another factor for Renault and Fiat to take into consideration.

Besides being involved through their trade unions and works

councils the workers in some companies have also been involved directly in formulating improvements – not as an alternative to their involvement through trade unions, but in ways which complement and reinforce it. As we have seen, the 'quality circles' at General Motors and the 'production' and 'development' groups at Saab are examples of ways in which people's ideas have been stimulated and put to constructive use.

But, as other aspects of what General Motors and Saab are doing show, there is more to direct involvement than the use of formal committees, although these committees can be helpful in getting the process going. At its best direct involvement is simply a matter of supervisors and line managers ensuring that those doing a job are always given the chance to play as full a part as they can in improving methods, and of design engineers always ensuring that they too consult production workers fully and at an early stage so that their ideas can be incorporated in the initial designs. This is rare. In many German plants design engineers now automatically ask production workers for their evaluation of any new methods and for their view of how what has been learnt can best be applied in the future. This is useful, but the best use of people's ideas and experience is made before, rather than after, a system is designed.

A survey commissioned by the European Foundation for the Improvement of Living and Working Conditions[3] illustrates some of the problems which can arise if workers are not fully involved early enough in the design process. For instance, control instruments are badly sited, breakdowns become unnecessarily frequent and operators complain of stress and frustration. The return on investment is not as high as it could be.

It is not just the design of technical systems that gives more scope for involving workers; in matters of work organization too there is scope to involve them more. Indeed the report suggests that many manufacturers could secure better return on investment by making more use of the opportunities that new technology offers to change the way work is organized. This would allow them to increase production flexibility still further as well as offering more scope for their employees to find satisfaction.

5. What happened as a result

What has resulted from all these changes in technology, job content, work organization and employee consultation? All the manufacturers cited above monitored results carefully and assessed their usefulness against criteria of economic competition. Some of these results were quantifiable. Others were not.

These were some of the quantifiable benefits frequently identified:

(i) Reduced labour turnover

This was common. In some cases the improvement was dramatic, and financial savings considerable, largely because of reduced training costs. For example, when other big employers in the Gothenburg area all recorded worsening figures for labour turnover, Volvo, during early work at the Lundby truck and bus plant, showed a fall in labour turnover from 50 per cent in 1969 to 12 per cent in 1972 and a further fall to 8 per cent a year later.

(ii) Reduced absenteeism

This was another common benefit. The example of General Motors' Tarrytown plant is important because the project was carried out during an extremely difficult economic and social situation. It involved almost 4,000 workers in a plant that was notorious for its problems, with poor industrial relations and high production costs. The project consisted almost entirely of involving the workers more fully in decisions both at plant and company level. Although little changed in the nature of the monotonous long-line assembly work, nevertheless the rate of absenteeism fell from $7\frac{1}{4}$ per cent to between 2 and 3 per cent over the seven years of the project, bringing financial savings through a reduced need for manning to cover such absences.

The figures from Saab and Volvo are significant too because in Sweden absenteeism was a catastrophically expensive problem. Saab found that absenteeism fell from 30 per cent to around 12 per cent during the first year of using group assembly in their new petrol engine plant. And after six years of operating their Kalmar plant Volvo[4] reported that absenteeism there is about half of that in their more traditional Torslanda plant.

Fiat also reported improvements, including an absenteeism rate of only 5 or 6 per cent at the new Cassino plant, compared with 12 or 13 per cent at the more traditional Turin plant.

(iii) Productivity and quality improved

General Motors' figures of inspection costs and returns by dealers show that Tarrytown climbed from being their worst plant before the project into the top group of their eighteen divisional plants. The plant that had been a thorn in everyone's flesh became a corporation showpiece.

Taking figures from a new plant Volvo estimate that man hours per car are between 10 and 15 per cent lower at Kalmar than at their more traditional Torslanda plant, with shorter assembly times and savings in time spent on indirect work such as planning, materials handling and quality control.

Such successes were not achieved without some problems in the early days. There were even examples of group assembly experiments being stopped because productivity targets were not being met: this happened in the case of some of Fiat's 'island' experiments and one early experiment in the motor caravan part of General Motors' truck and Coach Division. However, such cases were very much in the minority. Teething troubles were usually overcome and, overall, targets for both productivity and quality were met; the performance of the parts of the organizations which worked conventionally was improved on or at least equalled.

(iv) Manning requirements reduced

This benefit is less widely reported, but there are some examples. For instance, Volvo traditionally built in a 15 per cent requirement above standard level to cover rest breaks. This is not necessary in the new plants because the group members there substitute for each other to cover breaks. The new groups also require fewer supervisors. These reduced manning levels have not led to redundancies because people have either been redeployed elsewhere in the Company, or not recruited in the first place.

(v) Grievances reduced

This was not a factor in Sweden where industrial relations were already relatively stable, but Fiat management report that the new approach did help to improve relations with their militant trade unions. General Motors also report an improvement; at Tarrytown, for example, grievances fell from 2,000 per year around 1970 to only 32 in 1978.

Against these quantifiable benefits there were certain quantifiable costs:

(i) Wage costs rose slightly

This happened when people took on more skilled work which justified increased pay according to a wage system based on job evaluation. Increased wage costs were small – between 2 and 3 per cent was an early Volvo estimate – certainly no more than the developing skills justified.

(ii) Training costs increased slightly

It is difficult to estimate the exact extent of any increases in such costs. Costs rose because people needed to learn new skills. This was in effect an investment for the manufacturers, but against this has to be set lower training costs incurred as labour turnover reduced. Certainly none of the manufacturers were disturbed by any of the increased training costs which occurred.

(iii) New plants cost more than traditional ones

This was by far the most significant element in any increased costs. The specially designed plants with their excellent environments, greater space requirements, new technology and tooling, cost more to build and to equip than did traditional plants – about 10 per cent more in Volvo's estimate. But this amount is well within contingency for a new plant of that size, and the extra flexibility it offered more than offset the extra cost.

As well as looking at quantifiable costs and benefits manufacturers had to take into account results which are hard to express in figures. Indeed the need to monitor unquantified results has encouraged what is in many ways a new approach to evaluation and to accounting. The use of judgement by manager, employees and trade union representatives is crucial to this new approach. Judgement is a normal part of business, and certainly good judgement is accepted as the hallmark of the able manager and the successful entrepreneur, but nevertheless it takes courage deliberately to build it into an assessment of a vital commercial venture. Yet this is what manufacturers had to do. They could not realistically evaluate programmes which aimed at changing attitudes and behaviour without taking account of such qualitative evidence as how people were feeling and how this in turn affected their behaviour. There were intangible results on both the technical and social side and almost all of them were positive.

On the technical side the crucial factor was whether or not production flexibility had increased. This was, of course, reflected in statistics, but it was esentially a matter of the judgement of managers and supervisors. Had disruptions decreased? Were those that did occur being handled more effectively? Was rebalancing or adjustment to changes in requirements taking place more smoothly? In all cases the views of managers and supervisors supported the figures: the new methods did increase production flexibility – and that was what was most important.

The results in terms of relationships were especially important since it was changes in attitude – of operators, managers and trade union representatives – that would ultimately determine whether or not productivity and quality would improve. These results were also the least tangible and therefore the most difficult to assess. The nature of job satisfaction is notoriously elusive; it is very much an individual matter: a task that satisfies one person can bore another and yet overstretch a third. What is stimulating at the outset can become tedious as skills and expectations increase. An increase in involvement welcomed by one person, is interpreted by another as management failing to do its job and a change that makes a production worker feel that his job is more worthwhile can make his supervisor feel impoverished and threatened.

As well as how people feel there is the question of how they behave. Manufacturers had to assess how far any increased satisfaction or understanding led to increased commitment or improved communication, and whether these in turn led to higher productivity and better quality production.

These were the kind of considerations which guided manufacturers' attempts to gauge the extent and effects of changes in attitude. They made their assessments in various ways. For instance operators were often interviewed and asked to complete questionnaires and the views of their supervisors and trade union representatives were sought. Sometimes the results of questionnaires were fed back to participants and this feedback formed the basis of further interviews and discussions.

(i) Operators

Some problems emerged. There were instances of projects not going far enough, in which case it was often possible to extend them. There were also examples of projects going too far, too fast. At the BMW motorcycle assembly plant in Berlin, for instance, operators felt they were being overtaxed by individual jobs with cycles of 60 minutes. As a result these jobs were converted back to more relaxed assembly-line jobs with cycles of 15 to 20 minutes. Manufacturers learnt that such changes were best introduced gradually so that people had time to adapt.

In other cases changes which management and design engineers had expected to appeal had not done so, job rotation, for instance, was less welcomed than job enlargement and job enrichment. During the early stages at Saab some people welcomed job rotation while others actually resisted it even though in some cases they had proposed it themselves. Opel in Germany also found job rotation something of a problem. Two-thirds of one group were not prepared to take part in job rotation several times a day. And some IfaA (Institut für angewandte Arbeitswissenschaft) reports suggest that about 80 per cent of another group voted against job rotation after giving it a trial.

It also took time for operators to learn to behave differently. This was most evident when they were involved in meetings, whether with other operators, supervisors or technical experts. First they had to become convinced that their ideas were being seriously sought. Then they needed to learn how to contribute effectively. But, gradually, time-wasting and negative attitudes gave way to constructive discussion and, despite such teething troubles, the overall results were overwhelmingly positive. Operators welcomed the changes and few had any lasting difficulties in adjusting. They regarded the changes as manufacturers had hoped they would – as the chance to exercise more control over their lives – and out of this they derived satisfaction. A girl at Saab made a comment which sums up the general view: 'you feel more like a human being working in this way'.[5]

For this sort of reason people preferred the new way of working to the old, a preference that was particularly marked in new plants where manufacturers were able to introduce radical changes. Volvo, for instance, report that satisfaction with the Kalmar system of group working is higher than with traditional methods, even where these traditional methods have been modified.

General Motors found the same thing: specially conducted surveys of the 'quality of working life' show that 48 per cent of all industrial workers in the corporation as a whole think that their quality of working life is high. But in three new plants a much higher percentage expressed this satisfaction – 83 per cent, 84 per cent and 90 per cent respectively.

Companies are convinced that this increased satisfaction has been reflected in increased commitment to the job and to the company. Volvo summed it up by saying that at Kalmar an 'entrepreneurial spirit' has been created amongst the workforce – and that is behind the success of any enterprise.

(ii) Managers

All companies agreed that success would depend particularly on the attitude of their managers and supervisors. The management style they were seeking was characterized by qualities such as vitality; flexibility; willingness to take sensible risks and to learn from experience; and the ability to change from an authoritarian approach to one which is responsive to subordinates and which encourages them to take responsibility, use initiative and put forward ideas.

They found that it takes time for such abilities to develop. It was not always easy for managers and supervisors to grasp what was required of them and at the same time to grow out of familiar habits, particularly when they felt, as many did initially, that the kind of change required was personally threatening. This is a common problem, as the other case studies will demonstrate. But with more experience and appropriate training it did prove possible for most managers to adapt, some with alacrity, others with more hesitation.

Like the operators, managers and supervisors welcomed the changes. They saw the benefits to their subordinates and they also felt that their own jobs were made more stimulating. Far from the new approach undermining their authority, as some had feared, they found that it actually enhanced it. They saw themselves as better managers, more relaxed, but more in control of the situation – albeit a different kind of control. For their part, manufacturers felt they had gained not only more skilled operators, but also more skilled managers.

(iii) Trade union representatives

Most trade union representatives also valued the new approach, seeing the possibility of benefits to their members and in most cases representatives have welcomed the increased consultation that has resulted. They have also found that the increased involvement in operations that their members now enjoy has increased their involvement in trade union affairs. The new way of working, instead of undermining their position, as some trade union representatives feared it would, has actually extended their influence, involving them in new areas beyond the scope of traditional collective bargaining and bringing them a more active membership.

But not all trade union representatives were content. Even amongst the many who were satisfied with the general direction of change there were those who felt that manufacturers could and should go still further, giving people more scope to use and develop their skills, influence what goes on from day to day and shape their future. Dissatisfaction of this kind is perhaps greatest in Italy where, much as the unions value the tangible benefits of the new technology, they still feel that management have not yet released enough of their traditional power and prerogatives.

The effect on industrial relations was subtle. Some companies, such as General Motors and Fiat, point to a reduction in disputes, but for most the results were intangible. In most companies where management and trade unions have gone through the process of change together, mutual understanding and trust have tended to grow as a result. But this did not mean that either side abandoned traditional responsibilities. Trade union representatives did not become compliant tools of management nor did management give way to the trade unions when they felt it would be irresponsible to do so. The conflict did not go out of industrial relations, but both sides developed the ability to tolerate differences of aim and view and to prevent these from obstructing progress.

Overall Assessment

Taken overall, manufacturers are convinced that the new approach is the right one. In their judgement it is commercially cost-effective. Even the higher costs of purpose-built plants like Kalmar and Skövde can be completely offset by the resulting benefits.

They stress that, although they must go on learning, the new approach is no longer 'experimental', it is now a matter of continuing to develop an operating strategy and to implement it as efficiently as possible. As one Volvo representative said, 'we shall never build another Kalmar, successful though it is. We have learnt from it and we shall try to do something even better next time.' Equally important, they stress that even if they had found the overall costs of the new approach to be higher, they would still have wished to pursue it for the benefits it offers, so convinced are they that it is no longer commercially feasible to make cars by unmodified traditional methods.

5 The Italian metal working industry

1. Background

The relationship between organized labour and management is one of the most important influences on the success of attempts to improve an organisation's performance. Therefore I have included a case study which focuses on this relationship. The examples I have chosen come from Italy, a country where the role of industrial relations in organizational change is particularly significant. Managers, trade unionists and advisers can, I believe, learn a good deal from what has happened there, not by treating what Italian companies have done as examples to be copied, but simply by looking at their experience, always bearing in mind that certain features are peculiar to the Italian scene.

First, there are, to all intents and purposes, only three trade unions that matter (in marked contrast, for instance, to the UK). These account for around 99 per cent of all trade union members.

Second, these major unions are differentiated not along craft lines, but politically. Thus the largest, CGIL (Confederazione Generale Italiana del Lavoro), is essentially Marxist/Communist. The next largest, CISL (Confederazione Italiana Sindacati Lavoratori), began after the Second World War as a liberal/conservative, anti-communist 'Christian' union. Since then it has moved further to the left. The third union, UIL (Unione Italiana Lavoratori), was originally 'centre', although it has been regarded by trade union representatives as being 'more management than workers . . . more right than centre'. Recently, however, it has been moving further left as many left wing Socialists have been joining it with the intention, some say, of making it 'the union of the Socialist party'.

Third, despite these political differences, the three major unions have since the late 1960s agreed common policies and have presented a united front in negotiation with management at all levels.

Lastly, the trade unions have identified organizational change as one of their most important objectives. They do not, however, see improvements in working conditions and job satisfaction as an end in themselves, but rather as a starting point, a necessary precondition for their programme of social and political change. The growth in workers' control which would result from their involvement in decisions at the place of work would, the unions feel, lead ultimately to even greater workers' control, political as well as industrial.

Such objectives are not, of course, shared by Italian management, and in many organizations this divergence has been a barrier to change. However, in certain significant companies impressive progress has been made – and it is where the trade unions have been best organized and most militant that the achievements have been greatest. The cases I have chosen (Olivetti; Fiat; Italsider, the State-owned steel company; and Graziano, a manufacturer of lathes) are, therefore, all taken from the metal working sector where the trade unions are most strongly organized.

2. The problems faced

The 1960s in Italy saw a growing concern for the quality of working life, but few active attempts to improve it. By the early 1970s the concern had culminated in what one Italian consultant called a 'fashionable ideology' accompanied by a good deal of project activity which, while widespread, was largely undiscriminating or superficial. Most of this activity was curtailed during the economic, social and political crises of the mid-1970s, leaving in existence only the more coherent and comprehensive programmes for change.

These more significant programmes have taken place in some of the most successful Italian companies like Fiat, Olivetti, Italsider, as well as in a few smaller, far-sighted organizations like Graziano. What marks out these attempts to introduce change is that they were undertaken not in response to fashion, but for compelling practical reasons which sprang from three main sources: the employees, the trade unions and the market.

(i) The employees

In Italy, as in other industrial countries, the late 1960s were, as one manager put it, 'times of deep social change'. This familiar state of affairs was reinforced in Italy by a relatively high proportion of better-educated young people entering the labour market than ever before – an outcome both of Italy's relatively high birth-rate and of the raising, in 1962, of the minimum school-leaving age. The result was a better-educated workforce composed of individuals who expected both more interesting jobs and what one industrial relations specialist called more 'self-determination of what they do and how they increase their skills, get promotion and so on'. The new workforce would no longer tolerate what had been accepted previously, neither in the nature of the work, nor its environment. Their dissatisfaction was reflected in growing absenteeism, high labour turnover and militancy. Initially many managers were reluctant to take this dissatisfaction seriously, seeing it as a problem artificially created and intensified by the trade unions but employers found that this dissatisfaction persisted even after the economic crisis made employment more difficult to obtain.

There was, too, a peculiarly Italian factor seen as important by both managers and trade unionists. The Italians have no ready source of foreign labour of low educational standard and aspirations. There were no temporary foreign workers, like Germany's 'Gastarbeiter', to take the least skilled, most exhausting jobs, only Italians. Some contend that for a time this pool of exploitable labour was supplied to the industrial North by the impoverished, agricultural South; but this effect could not last long, as all Italians are governed by essentially the same laws, exposed to the same information media and represented by the same trade unions.

The end result in the organizations we are considering was that management came to regard employees' dissatisfaction with their work and prospects as a pressing problem which had to be taken seriously. The reasons given for responding to employees' dissatisfaction vary, but two elements remained constant: 'business reasons' (high absenteeism and labour turnover are expensive), and 'humanitarian reasons', ranging from a growing conviction that 'it is not right to treat people like monkeys', as one Fiat manager said, to what a trade unionist called the 'far-sighted humanitarianism' of 'Utopian men' like the late Adriano Olivetti.

(ii) The trade unions

Although the question of how best to respond to changing employee attitudes had some peculiarly Italian twists, it was substantially the same problem which had confronted car manufacturers and other organizations in Western industrial countries since the 1960s. The problem of how best to respond to the quite considerable pressure from the Italian trade unions for this kind of change was, on the other hand, unique.

The strategy behind this trade union pressure has always been essentially practical. In the words of one national official, its aim is to stimulate the 'growth in workers' consciousness' and 'the growing refusal to accept a Tayloristic situation' which they feel has been evident since the social, industrial and political unrest of the late 1960s. Ultimately they intend the workers themselves to arrive at 'a political strategy for the development of their country'. Their conviction that this is necessary comes from their analysis of the Italian social, economic and political scene. As the unions see it, it has been possible, until the recent unrest, to 'use people without regard to their feelings'. Italians have tolerated low wages, poor housing and appalling public service and have allowed themselves to become 'the instruments of the capitalists'. In this way Italian capitalists have become rich, their wealth based on the cheap mass production of goods for the private consumer – cars, washing machines, refrigerators and so on – a form of production requiring relatively low investment in technology, especially where workers will tolerate poor working conditions.

Such a production process has lent itself to fragmented, machine-paced, assembly-line jobs, piece-work pay systems, and hierarchical organization structures which place control firmly in the hands of management. The workers are, as one trade union representative expressed it, 'the dependent variable'. If demand for the product increases they are called upon to work harder for longer hours, and if it decreases their wages are cut, they are shunted between departments or laid off. The unions feel that the Italian political system has reinforced this situation, particularly in the South where they see right wing power as the basis of under-development.

In the light of this analysis they conclude that 'working conditions' (a term which, to the Italians, embraces the way that work is organized, managed and rewarded, as well as physical conditions) 'cannot be changed without changing everything'. They go on to identify working conditions as 'the starting point' of their strategy for change. In practical terms their aim is to change the way work is organized and people are managed and rewarded so that the workers gain control of the production process and ultimately of decisions about the development of the organization. In this way they see working conditions as 'the key by which an individual can under-stand and criticize the general situation, the link between the indi-vidual and choices about the development of the country'.

It is this analysis and the resultant strategy which makes the Italian trade union movement unlike that of other countries. The French, for instance, and some British union officials, share the Italians' analysis, but not their strategy, feeling that there is little point in action until the political situation is substantially changed. (Some feel that the French government's move to the left in the early 1980s may make more trade union involvement possible.) The North American and many British trade unionists, on the other hand, are basically wedded to the capitalist system. The Scandinavian and German unions feel able to share in decisions with management in a way which the Italians rule out because they identify an essential conflict of interests.

The Italian trade unions have taken various practical steps in pursuit of their objectives. The strategy itself gave a new twist to disputes over traditional issues like wage levels, working hours, and the nature of pay systems. As well as pressure for increases of pay and reduction of hours, demands after 1968 began to reflect the unions' rejection of the link between wages and productivity and their insistence on what they call 'wage egalitarianism'. In particular they achieved a minimum payment for piece-work, independent of output; the setting of a maximum level of output beyond which piece-work payments would no longer be made; and the abolition of piece-work for unpleasant or dangerous work ('our health is not for sale'). Pro-duction bonuses were to be fixed and independent of actual output, and furthermore, the size of any bonus was to be the same for all workers, irrespective of grade. An annual maximum quota of over-time hours available to the organization from each worker was also set, and management accepted an obligation to explain the reasons for any overtime. Management also accepted restraints on their freedom to move workers between jobs and departments.

The overall effect of such changes was to reduce management control in two areas seen as crucial by the unions: their ability to 'manipulate' effort through the payment system; and their power to deploy the labour force in accordance with the company's production requirements. However, the most significant challenge to manage-ment's control of the way the work is organized came not from the unions' treatment of traditional negotiating issues, but rather from bringing new issues into the bargaining arena. The most significant of these were 'professionalism' and the grading of workers, and investment policy.

Agreements related to the grading of work (the 'single status' or 'Inquadramento Unico' agreements) are regarded by the unions as their most important means of achieving change. They greatly simplified the Italian pay and grading structure, reducing the number of job evaluation classifications normally used and placing all jobs, blue, white-collar and managerial, on a single continuum. They embody the unions' wish to move towards a more 'egalitarian' organization of work. They include general statements to the effect that employee skills 'should' be improved. Although they do not specify how this is to be achieved, the effect is to give each employee what the trade unions call 'the right to a career', to be trained to do, and given the opportunity to do, jobs which will enable him to move through the continuum as far as he is able. There is a limit to the length of time a worker can remain in one of the lower grades before being offered further training. Pay is linked to grade, but it reflects not only the job the employee is currently doing, but also what he is capable of, whether or not his current job uses these capabilities.

These agreements originated in a local agreement reached at Italsider in 1970, after considerable trade union pressure which culminated in a violent strike. It reduced the number of job evaluation grades by which work can be categorized from approximately 50 to 8, the lowest of which, level 1, seldom occurs in practice. All jobs in the company fit into this single classification. Levels 2 to 5 cover blue-collar work and levels 2 to 8 cover white-collar and managerial jobs: thus there is some overlap. This has become the pattern for the national agreement covering the metal working sector.

Similar collective agreements were reached at Fiat and Olivetti in 1971, where the number of blue-collar grades were also reduced to 4. In both cases the company undertook that workers should not remain in the lowest category (category 4) for more than 18 months. Promotion from the third to the second category was also regulated, specifying both the number of workers to be promoted and the time allowed for promotion. The agreements also state the methods to be used to ensure that promotion means not only more money, but also changes in job content – more responsibility, more interest, more skilled work and so on. The companies had to ensure that employees received the training necessary to prepare them for more skilled work.

Altogether the agreements mean that changes in the organization or method of working are subject to collective bargaining and they have been a powerful impetus towards change in the metal working industry where the unions are well organized. Agreements on the same lines have since been concluded in all other major sectors of the economy. However, even in the metal working sector they have not, by themselves, provided a sufficient lever for the unions to achieve the egalitarianism and control at which they aim. A more recent series of national agreements concluded in 1976 took the unions a step further. These related to investment and employment policy and obliged employers to inform the unions, before a decision is taken, of any change which will affect what the trade unions call the 'quality of employment' – for instance, new technology or processes, changes in training, hours, the utilization of the workforce and investment possibilities. The unions' aim in pushing for these agreements was to gain for themselves some control over investment programmes and so force companies to take into account the interests of workers, both employed and unemployed. But agreements alone do not bring about changes of attitude and the unions are still some way from achieving the control they want. None the less, the agreements do represent another threat to management's traditional decision-making powers.

Important though these formal agreements are in the unions' strategy, they have by no means been seen as the only way ahead. 'Informal' action of less easily defined kinds has been vital too and here the unions regard what they call 'the problem of structures' as crucial. Their aim is to build up, within an establishment, an effective system of representation which would enable workers to control all decisions which affect them. Under a system of representation still relatively new in Italy each natural working group, or 'homogeneous group', has its own representative. These representatives, who might or might not be trade union members, are elected freely by all workers, both members and non-members. Each representative typically represents between thirty and fifty workers. There is no fixed time of election or term of office. They hold office for as long as those they represent wish them to and then change accordingly. These representatives sit on works council committees (the Consiglio di Fabrica) with management representatives at plant level and in large plants at departmental level.

Union leaders regard these workers' representatives on the Consiglio within a plant as shop stewards and contend that they constitute the official organizing body for trade union activity. (In the later

1970s, however, workers began claiming the right to act independently of this body and other union representatives if they wish. It is too early to say how this break with union discipline, a trend which national officials do not officially recognize, will turn out.)

The unions feel that this system offers certain advantages since the workers see their representative as 'their man' rather than 'the union's man'. This can be important, especially where union membership is low. However, it also presents problems which they have been trying to overcome. Not only is there the risk of an alternative and competing representation system, but also the danger that non-union shop stewards will take a narrow view, being 'more interested in their factory than in the whole working class'. The unions' solution is to 'recognize' the shop steward as the official representative of the workers, whether or not he is a trade union member, even going so far as to say that at plant level 'the network of shop stewards is the union'. Once a steward is in office the unions, 'of course, try to influence him to persuade him to accept the wider view'.

Providing they make some impact here, the unions see many advantages to the new system in terms of their overall strategy. The 'homogeneous groups' and the individuals in them provide the basic structure for the workers' control at which they aim. These people have a direct understanding of the work they do and the conditions in which they do it. Therefore, contend the unions, they, together with their shop steward, are well equipped to analyse their situation and make claims designed to improve both their physical conditions and the control they have over day to day matters.

In practice, therefore, the unions have been trying to strengthen the shop steward's role in every way; for instance, by insisting that management supply production information not normally shared and that they disaggregate it, supplying it separately for each working group. Thus the steward and his group can understand management decisions and are better able to resist management attempts to 'exploit' them in the way they deploy resources and set production times.

To broaden the area of workers' control the unions feel it is vital that workers within a plant establish links with the wider working (and non-working) community. They have been trying to achieve this both by increasing union influence over the company's decisions which affect wider groups (the 1976 agreements on investment decisions were especially important here) and by working in local communities. The aim of the latter is to increase the influence that the public, rather than the central administration, has over local matters. For instance, legislation passed in spring 1977 gave new decision-making powers to the eighteen Italian regions over matters such as housing, agriculture, public works, schools, hospitals etc. The unions plan to encourage people to use this opportunity.

Even before this legislation there were examples of local participation, albeit patchy. The most significant have been in the 'reform' of the hospital and school systems. For instance, legislation requiring public involvement in decisions related to school administration and teaching methods has been passed. The unions have themselves taken part at local level and they have been encouraging what is often an apathetic public to do the same. They have also been using the opportunity presented by 'the 150 hours' law, which entitles all workers to a significant period of time off work each year to study at their employer's expense, to try to influence schooling so that it provides a suitable preparation for the type of working life at which they are aiming.

The policy of using organizational change – or 'improving working conditions' as the Italians tend to call it – as the keystone of their strategy of increasing the political control in the hands of workers has guided the efforts of Italian trade union officials for some years, particularly at national level. But in the shorter term they have had other related objectives, especially at regional and plant level. For instance, the current economic crisis has focused trade union attention on maintaining employment. Some say that working to save jobs has made them more inclined to co-operate with management, but leading trade union officials would disagree. They see maintaining employment as another issue over which workers should increase their control. Accordingly they say that if there are to be 'sacrifices', and they feel this is inevitable, then the trade unions must determine what they should be. In this way they can use 'austerity' to reduce management's discretion over jobs and pay and to help the trade unions towards their main aim of transforming economic and social structures.

(iii) The market

These trade union strategies have been criticized by many as being over-ambitious, politically unacceptable, inconsistent and impractical. But, whatever one's point of view, it must be said that the determined and ingenious efforts of trade unionists have had considerable influence on Italian management. However, it would be quite wrong to give the impression that management have been pushed against their will into making changes. Indeed in many cases it seems more likely that strain in industrial relations and distrust of the unions have led management to disregard valid reasons for change in an instinctive reaction against this kind of union pressure. But not all; Olivetti, Graziano, Italsider and Fiat identified compelling commercial and technical reasons for change which took them in the same direction as that of the unions, but for very different reasons. Management in these companies wanted change, but wanted it in order to make the profit necessary for survival.

The production methods of all these companies involved either traditional assembly lines or, in the case of Italsider, the steel manufacturer, other conventional processes broadly equivalent to assembly lines. Such methods were insufficiently flexible for the economic manufacture of the type of products increasingly wanted by customers. For instance, Olivetti customers began to require electronic, in preference to mechanical, office equipment. Because electronic machines are built up from a range of possible modules they could not be competitively produced on assembly lines. Customers increasingly demanded a machine designed to meet their individual requirements and here, too, assembly lines were impractical because their inflexibility meant that they could only economically produce uniform machines. The new processes, which were necessary to make the new products, required people with special skills, and managers in the various companies foresaw the need for more training and development. For instance, the majority of the assembly line workers at Graziano, accustomed to making conventional lathes, were insufficiently skilled as things stood to build the automatic lathes increasingly required by customers.

Italsider were concerned about 'the sensitivity' of the new automated steel making processes which had to be introduced if they were to remain competitive. New forms of controlling the process became necessary, more dependent than before on the skill and initiative of the workers. Previously the workers had been largely unskilled labourers. They had to become not only technically more skilled, but also able to work well together in groups, to communicate accurately and to use their own and each other's experience to the full. The job-evaluated grading systems introduced into the Italian metal working sector through the Inquadramento Unico agreements of the early 1970s, provided an excellent framework for coping with such increases in skills. Consequently the whole upgrading process was able to progress relatively smoothly. Certainly there was some fierce bargaining, but it did not tend to be so time-consuming and unpredictable as it often is, for example, in the UK where there are many more trade unions involved and a less appropriate framework.

The need to change did pose problems, but the very magnitude of the pressure for change had certain advantages. As one Olivetti manager observed, his opposite numbers in non-profit making organizations, or in those whose production processes involved little technology would be just as likely to be under pressures to change, from customers as well as from employees and their trade unions. But since their problems might lack the same clarity – and were therefore not viewed with the same urgency as those at Olivetti – he felt that their true nature might be concealed. It would be easy for such managers to be lulled into a sense of false security and to avoid coming to terms with their crucial problems.

3. The changes made

Against this background Olivetti, Italsider, Graziano, and Fiat all focused on working methods, adapting them sometimes quite radically so that they would:

(i) allow employees more scope to use their abilities and acquire new skills which would equip them for promotion to higher level work;

(ii) increase production workers' responsibility for and control over ancillary functions, such as training and quality control;

(iii) accommodate new technology and improve the working environment.

Taken together these changes created a completely new working environment. Employees not only gained greater control over their working lives from day to day but, also, those capable of advancement were guaranteed opportunities for career development. Employers, for their part, gained increased production flexibility and an in-built means of increasing the skills of their workforce – both of which they required if they were to keep pace with changing demands from their customers.

Although the principles underlying what was done were similar in all these companies, the changes themselves took a variety of forms. Graziano and Olivetti moved from assembly on lines to assembly by groups on fixed stations or islands ('*isola*'). Day-to-day production scheduling, training and quality control are now all left to team members, the supervisor providing any support for which the group asks. The aim, as an Olivetti manager described it, is to 'bring back the skill and pride of the artisan'.

Thus at Graziano each assembly line which previously made a lathe has been replaced by about seven groups of between five and six workers. Each group has become fully responsible for one stage of manufacture, such as the headstock assembly. Each group knows the timings to be met to ensure economic production. Having been told of the production requirements by its supervisor, members decide who will do what tasks; how they will rotate; how they will fit in training, cover sickness, breaks and so on. Each group is responsible for the quality of what it produces, and carries out any checks members feel to be necessary, as well as a final check when the assembly stage is completed. Group members must also ensure that all the parts they need are available at the right time. They are helped in this by the supply department which tends to anticipate these needs and so ensure smooth delivery.

Each worker can request transfer to another group so that he can develop his skills by learning other kinds of work. Typically such requests come after between one and two years in a group. It will probably take between eight and ten years for a worker to become skilled over all the different functions – quite an achievement because the skills required are 'informal' as well as formal or technical.

The role of the supervisor has been profoundly affected by these alterations. Previously he spent most of his time dealing with day-to-day operational problems – like how to cover for absenteeism and so on – which are now the responsibility of the groups. As one supervisor said, the job is now 'far less tangible'. He is ultimately responsible for the quality of what is produced by the six or seven groups that report to him (broadly equivalent to those making a complete lathe) and this is difficult to define in concrete terms.

Of all Italian companies, perhaps Olivetti has taken the greatest interest in innovations of this kind, so much so that the organization of work has gradually been transformed for the majority of its employees. When their products were mainly mechanical, Olivetti had a strongly centralized organization structure with production and ancillary tasks (like quality control, training and supply of material and parts) being fairly rigidly separated, even at foreman level. The manufacturing process itself created fragmented jobs which required little skill; rewarded quantity rather than quality on an individual piece-work basis; and offered little prospect of acquiring the new skills which would lead to professional advancement.

The change-over to production of the electronic products increasingly demanded by customers made new work methods and organization structures imperative. This change-over did not take place all at once, but through a variety of stages. The principles underlying this transformation were:

(i)   integrating production and quality control, as far as possible at all levels;

(ii) strengthening links between production and the supply of materials and parts;

(iii) making the assembly group responsible for the organization and methods of production, basically by building it into the foreman's role (previously organization and methods had been the responsibility of those outside production, notably the engineers: as one manager said, 'before we used to concentrate on times. Now we encourage the groups to improve methods and allow improvements in times to follow.').

Nowadays the typical pattern is that small groups ('integrated assembly units') of workers on fixed stations, or 'islands', assemble either whole products or a coherent part, or 'module', of a complete item. Job rotation, ordering the necessary parts, carrying out much of the quality control and testing – or at least liaising closely with the inspectors – all offer group members the chance to acquire the new skills necessary for advancement. Incentives are based on the work of the group, not on the output of individuals and they reward quality and regularity of output, not just quantity.

Such changes have implications for organization structure and for jobs ancillary to the manufacturing process; quality control, for instance, is now closely integrated with production. The supply of materials and parts is also more closely linked to production. The complex task of supplying the thousands of parts required to the integrated assembly units is indeed crucial. Mistakes mean 'great disruption' with its attendant waste of time and money, and to prevent this Olivetti have enriched the jobs of the supply clerks. Previously responsibility was divided 'vertically' between the clerks, each clerk dealing with one part. Now it is divided 'horizontally'. Clerks work in pairs, between them supplying all the parts needed to assemble a complete product, one of them 'looking to the factories which supply Olivetti with the parts, the other to the groups which use them'. Thus they are more closely linked than before to a group of workers and its foreman and so they have a direct relationship with their internal 'customers'.

But, as at Graziano, the greatest changes at Olivetti have been in the role of the foreman. He now has overall responsibility for the quality and smoothness of production, an 'intangible' task which needs greater interpersonal as well as technical skills than were required under the more traditional assembly-line methods.

Fiat too have tested island assembly, notably at Rivalta, their body assembly facility near Turin, and at Termoli, their engine assembly plant in Southern Italy. During these tests assembly took place not on lines, but on a series of islands composed of a varying number of work stations. Each worker became responsible for completing a particular operation, typically equivalent to two or more assembly-line jobs. Consequently job cycle times were increased, for instance to about fourteen minutes at Termoli. As each work-piece is stationary the worker's rhythm was no longer predetermined by line speed. Further flexibility was provided by 'buffer stocks' of semi-finished products between the various islands. However, unlike Graziano and Olivetti, Fiat did not enrich jobs or change organization by integrating ancillary functions like quality control or training. Essentially Fiat were using job enlargement. They have not, to date, had the same success with island assembly as have Graziano and Olivetti and, accordingly, the technique is only a minor and strictly experimental aspect of their innovations.

Fiat have been more successful with modifying assembly lines. They have made some use of job rotation, job enlargement and job enrichment in existing plants, but, not surprisingly, most scope has been offered in new plants. For instance, at the new plant at Cassino in the South they chose to install four slow-speed lines for final assembly offering job cycle times of around four minutes instead of the traditional long lines, which had a typical cycle time of around one minute (as we saw in the last chapter). As a result jobs were made less repetitive and production flexibility greatly increased. Further advances were made in engine assembly at their Mirafiori plant. Here short lines were broken by buffer stores to increase production flexibility and operator choice still further.

However, the main thrust of Fiat's innovations are undoubtedly in automation, eliminating tedious and dangerous jobs like operating presses, painting and welding. The most important advance in welding, for instance, is the use at Rivalta and Cassino of the 'Robogate' process for body framing on the Ritmo/Strada (as described in the car industry case study). Fiat are also working on automating assembly. Here their most important innovation has been in the use of the computer-controlled Digitron process to achieve the marriage of body and power train on the Fiat 131. The car and the process were specially designed for each other and Fiat's experience of using the process has led them to anticipate good results on future models. (This process is also described in the car industry case study.)

At Italsider too the need to introduce new technology was the most powerful impetus to innovation, but in this case the resulting changes went further and deeper than at Fiat. Action began slowly at Italsider around 1970. Their early projects were all confined to small areas of certain plants and were limited to specific problems, like safety, rather than focused directly on redesigning jobs and changing the organization. But although these early projects were limited, they were significant. They demonstrated, particularly to the internal research team responsible, that 'it was not even possible to do something like improving safety without changing the organization of work. Once workers' behaviour changes, work organization must change too'.

It took some time for the researchers to convince management and the trade unions that more radical experiments directly related to organization change were now required. However, in 1974 such work did begin both in Genoa and Taranto, looking initially at the reorganization of work. The workers themselves carried out the analysis of the existing situation and identified the problems requiring solution. This proved to be a breakthrough. Success gave momentum to participative 'action research' of this kind and when, in 1975, it became necessary to replace two of the furnaces in Genoa with more sophisticated technology, Italsider decided to use the participative approach already developed.

Their aim was ambitious: to build up the new plants within the existing building while at the same time maintaining full production. In this way Italsider hoped to achieve savings which could be offset against their investment costs. Furthermore they planned to involve all nine hundred workers who would be affected by the change-over both in designing the new technology and work organization and in deciding how the changes would be implemented. To achieve this aim the internal 'action research' team suggested setting up various kinds of groups, each with a different role, which would involve between them foremen, managers, shop-stewards, technicians, safety experts, doctors, plant designers and the internal researchers themselves.

For instance, the project was managed by a multi-disciplinary 'steering group'. Beneath this group, 'analysis groups' composed of blue-collar workers from the plant were given the task of examining the proposed design and introduction of the new facilities both from the technical and social point of view. Complementing the analysis groups were 'seminar groups' involving virtually all nine hundred workers. The aim of these groups was not just to give the workers the technical knowledge they would require to operate the new plant, but also to help them to take part in designing it.

The project was a great success and the same kind of process has since been used elsewhere, for instance in the building of a new rolling mill in Genoa. (See Section 5, 'What happened as a result', for details of outcomes.) Such projects have led to more satisfying and more highly graded work for operators and different kinds of jobs for their foremen. The operators developed from mere labourers to skilled technicians with the opportunity to acquire greater 'social knowledge' and to learn to work together more effectively, 'exchanging their experience and enriching each other's expertise', in the words of one internal adviser. For the shift-foreman it meant a new role too. Previously his 'control' function was all-important, but, as 'control' became an inseparable part of the operators' job, the 'strategical, technical and research aspects' of the foreman's job were strengthened.

But those at Italsider stress that, important though these changes in job functions were, the crucial transformation has been in the position of the workers within the company. Both in carrying out his day-to-day tasks and in the design of new facilities the 'worker' is beginning to be seen as 'the expert'. The 'action research' process was the essential stimulus to this development.

4. How the changes were made

The process of introducing change in Italy is distinctive and very much influenced by the nature of the country's industrial relations.

Management, trade union representatives and professional advisers have each played their part.

The role of management

Essentially the pattern is for management to make proposals and for the trade unions to react to them through the normal bargaining machinery. This is so even though much of the pressure for change has come from employees and their representatives. In practice such pressure has been manifested in the form of 'general demands for improvement', and in various forms of industrial action, including strikes or, more passively, high rates of absenteeism. It has been left to management to respond by making specific proposals, either for alternative forms of organization or for new working methods. Thus the initiative has nearly always come from management. Proposals affecting blue-collar workers then become the subject of negotiation; when white-collar workers are affected, management tend instead to discuss their proposals with the individual job holder because, as one manager said, 'the unions' power does not extend there'.

The role of the unions

It may seem surprising that the unions are content to allow management the initiative in an area to which they have assigned so much political significance. There are two reasons for this. First the unions lack experience in handling what is a complex and still relatively new issue. So far they have preferred 'to declare for better conditions', leaving it to management to work out the details. However, the unions are becoming more reluctant to 'leave it to the intellectuals'. Consequently they are using outside advisers to train their officials and representatives in analysing operational problems and in formulating solutions. There are now, in the Milan area for instance, several examples of projects initiated by trade unions.

Second – and this is the main reason for their reluctance to play a more positive role – they see their political ideology as precluding them from any form of 'co-determination' with management. In reaching this view the unions have been heavily influenced by the Marxist philosophy of CGIL, the largest and most powerful union in the metal working sector. Thus, as a leading full-time official said, 'the Italian unions prefer to experiment with forms of workers' control through many channels, not through representative committees or participating with management, but through the negotiation process'. This, they feel, gives the workers greater influence, especially over 'complex issues like investment'.

It gives the unions an essentially adversarial role. As one Director of Industrial Relations said, 'the effect is that the Italian labour movement has only one way of posing problems and that is through conflict. To them accepting joint management means the acceptance of a system they always say they want to change'. Such political considerations are, however, chiefly the concern of full-time trade union officials, especially those at national and regional level. Within plants the picture is not so clear-cut. The main concern of many ordinary employees is simply to take on more skilled and interesting work and to increase their wages. Thus they – and their shop stewards – concentrate on practical change as it affects them personally, rather than on wider socio-political questions.

However, these people are not involved in the crucial plant level negotiations, which are often complicated. While the trade unions will not join with management in formulating proposals for change, they by no means oppose change. Rather they seek to channel it towards their own ends. Their aim is to reach agreements which will not only improve pay and conditions, give workers more control over working methods and the chance to take on more demanding work, but which will also be relevant to wider socio-political issues. Organizational change thus proceeds through negotiation; both sides want it, but bargain fiercely over the practical details, since each wants it as a means to different ends.

Although this is the general pattern there have been cases of a more genuinely participative approach. The most impressive example is the recent work at Italsider. Here the most important methodological principle has always been the full involvement of management, trade unions and workers in the design as well as the implementation of change. Initially it proved difficult to realise this aim since both management and unions were suspicious of each other. However, more recently, the use of joint steering committees and joint management/ union working groups has been paying dividends. For instance, the areas, goals and form of experimentation are now jointly decided. This means that projects can now be designed to meet the needs of all the different groups concerned and can draw on the experience of managers and specialists, of the workers doing the job, and of the trade unions who represent them. The pay and grading implications of the agreed changes are then subject to collective bargaining as elsewhere.

The role of the adviser

Most of these companies have used internal and external consultants to work with them on their projects and at Olivetti and Italsider the role of these advisers has been especially important. Inevitably the advisers' role is very much concerned with industrial relations. They do not take part in bargaining as such – this is entirely the province of management, trade union officials and workers' representatives. Their function is to help each side to understand the other side's legitimate interests and to cope rationally with the disagreements which arise, so that progress is not constantly interrupted by irrelevant conflict. As one Italsider adviser put it 'we are the vaseline'.

All the advisers I have met indicated that worthwhile change cannot be achieved without the full involvement of those affected. In practice this means that the advisers must be concerned with more than the negotiation process, vital though this is. As one senior internal consultant at Olivetti put it: 'We need to accept that the old, traditional ways of organizing work are not productive, not rational. Change cannot just be the product of industrial relations. It must be the product of rational decision. We must change the way of making these decisions and involve people at every level.' Equally, all agreed there could be no simple 'formula' or 'model' for such involvement and they are experimenting with different options. One leading external adviser who has worked both with Olivetti and Italsider feels that because 'it does not fit the Italian industrial relations situation' joint management/union design of new organization and jobs should be avoided. Instead, he proposes that both management and the trade unions should carry out their own organization analysis, covering all aspects of the organization, work methods, control systems, worker/management relationships etc. No limits should be placed on the changes proposed and practical details of change can then be settled through negotiation.

As he describes it, the role of the adviser is to 'train both sides so that they can make their own analysis, not to do it for them'. This method has apparently had 'great impact' on the trade unions who in certain cases are now enthusiastically and effectively pursuing their own research projects. The internal consultants at Italsider have always aimed to 'help management and the trade unions to develop a means of building a new type of work organization'. The main problem that the advisers have encountered – in common with many advisers elsewhere – is the confusion and anxieties which projects of this kind arouse on both sides.

What the Italsider advisers do to try to overcome this problem is to create a framework that gives people from both sides first hand knowledge of what is going on and direct involvement in it. In this way they build up understanding, which is the only effective weapon against disturbing rumours.

This is most easily achieved within plants where joint management/union steering committees have been set up to co-ordinate and direct experimental work. Reporting to them are 'analysis' groups composed of workers (selected by management and the unions) whose task it is to recommend changes in the light of their understanding of the situation. The changes agreed by the steering committee are then subject to collective bargaining. Thus management and the unions at plant level are able to influence the process of change through involvement in the design of proposals and the monitoring of progress, as well as through negotiation.

The Italsider advisers also have an important responsibility towards higher management and trade union officials outside the plant. It is more difficult to keep these people directly in touch with the progress of projects and as a result it is easy for them to misunderstand what is happening and to become anxious about it. There is then the risk that they may be tempted to intervene in a counter-productive way. It is part of the advisers' role to help them see that the success of projects depends on allowing negotiation to take place at the level of those closest to the problem. For instance, in the Genoa project (described above) only those within the plant had sufficient technical knowledge to determine what should be done.

All the advisers, internal and external, concerned with the projects described here, stressed the need for a clearer idea of exactly what changes projects should aim to create. The crux of the matter is what Italians call 'the real organization': the effective, co-operative way of working which develops spontaneously when people are free to determine for themselves how they should do their jobs, organize control systems and share out work. Italian advisers are trying to come to grips with this deceptively simple idea so that the conditions favourable to its development can be more effectively created.

5. What happened as a result

Assessment of results is a continuous process; managers look at them in terms of economic criteria and trade union representatives view them according to how far their members' needs are being met and their political and social objectives achieved. But evaluation of this kind of work inevitably presents difficulties: traditional measures have proved inadequate not only for assessing intangible benefits, such as the flexibility and improved motivation of workers, but also for the more tangible economic benefits. 'You cannot', said one Italsider adviser, 'mismatch methods of evaluation to these projects. You cannot use old measures for the new situation. Tonnage per person per hour is not good enough.'

So both sides have been trying to assess progress by new means but, like their counterparts in motor manufacturing, they have found that, as well as using objective measures, they have to rely on their judgement. On this basis both management and the trade unions are sufficiently convinced of the value of the new approach to want to go ahead, each for their own reasons.

Economic benefits

Despite measurement problems all the companies concerned could identify economic benefits. The most significant was the greatly increased flexibility of the new systems which enabled them to cope with changes in production programmes more quickly and cheaply. 'We can just add more assembly units', said one Olivetti manager, 'and retrain without disturbing people working on production.' It was also possible to reduce the amount of work in progress, thereby cutting costs and enabling a faster response to be made to to orders received by commercial departments. Quality also tended to improve and rates of error to decline, in some cases by as much as 85 per cent. Under island assembly at Graziano and Olivetti, where workers were responsible for correcting their own faults, it became rare for any defects found at final testing to be directly attributable to the assembly workers.

There were, of course, increased costs to be set against these benefits. The new methods tended to require more space, a problem experienced particularly at Fiat. Also investment in technology tended to be higher. Training costs increased as workers' courses became longer and more complex – up to 300 hours, for instance, on some Olivetti products, and quite considerable at Italsider too where, for instance in the Genoa project, all nine hundred workers received enough technical training to enable them to contribute to the design of new plants. Wage costs increased too, both because workers were taking on more skilled, and therefore higher graded work, and because as quality improved they earned higher incentive bonuses.

But these specific increased costs were by no means a problem in terms of total unit cost. They were partly offset by savings in indirect labour (for instance of between 20 and 30 per cent at Olivetti). The main point is that, far from being 'inflationary', such costs were simply regarded as just recognition for the higher skills and greater flexibility of the workforce.

These higher skills not only gave the benefit of improved production flexibility and quality, they also brought companies the benefit of technical suggestions from their workers. For instance, the design engineers at Italsider had no practical experience of actually working in a steel mill and could not, therefore, even envisage some of the problems which the workers not only identified, but also solved – like the fact that the design of the structure housing one of the furnaces was seventeen metres too short to allow efficient flow of materials or proper operation of the equipment. It is difficult to carry out cost benefit analyses which incorporate intangible factors such as these, but where these analyses were possible the newer methods were found to be more economic – for instance by between 10 and 20 per cent at Olivetti.

Employee attitudes

The way employees felt about the changes was clearly crucial in determining whether or not they were viable and each of the four companies attempted, by discussion and attitude survey, to assess people's feelings. In all cases the overall view was favourable, both because people found their new jobs were more interesting and gave them more control over the way their work was organized and because they appreciated the increased opportunities for gaining higher professional qualifications, promotion and pay. As one Fiat manager said, it is hard to assess how far this favourable view was due to 'actual appreciation of the change itself' and how far to 'personal considerations like the associated pay and promotion prospects'. In one sense this distinction does not matter. The crucial question is whether or not the workers would like to revert to former methods. The overwhelming answer was that they would not like to revert, despite initial problems of adjustment in some cases.

The companies also had to ask whether the changes improved motivation. It seemed that they did. Problems were not eliminated, but this was not expected. The important achievement as an Olivetti adviser described it was that the problems 'moved to a more rational level'.

Although demands for wage and grade improvements remained a live problem, workers 'no longer look for high pay as revenge' against a company which provides them with 'humiliating' work. Absenteeism decreased and some companies, like Olivetti for instance, noticed that the 'psychological and psychosomatic disorders usually associated with stress' declined.

Management's attitudes

Although the overall impression of management and employees was favourable, 'mistakes were inevitable, as in all human processes', as one Fiat manager said. Just as workers found some difficulty in adapting to 'the higher responsibilities of team working' although with training, support and experience this was usually overcome, so some managers found it difficult to adapt, particularly at lower and middle levels, where the changes in role tended to be most profound. For instance, the internal advisers at Italsider encountered 'confusion in the role of management at all levels when change is built up from below, but especially amongst supervisors'. Their previous role was that of 'control', a function which under the new system tends to be performed by a combination of more sophisticated equipment and more highly skilled workers. Supervisors, with their wider experience and expertise, are still very much needed under the new system when major problems arise, but it is hard for a supervisor to envisage this in advance of experiencing it. So anxiety seems to be inevitable, and is indeed widespread wherever such changes are introduced.

Problems of adjustment experienced by management have, on occasion, led to projects being abandoned. For instance, the Italsider advisers described one of their earlier projects in which, 'although every kind of reason was given' for the halt 'the real reason was that to change the work organization meant to change the power structure'. It would have meant allowing groups of workers to make decisions hitherto reserved for themselves by the managers. However, in general such fears gradually diminished as managers became accustomed to their own new role and learnt from experience that the workers were capable of fulfilling theirs.

The vital question for management is whether or not the new methods helped them meet the changing needs of customers more effectively. It is, of course, very difficult to assess the part the new methods have played, but the general view is that they were essential in maintaining the enterprises' viability. Precise figures are hard to come by, but this example from Olivetti provides some indication of the value of the new production methods. In 1964 (before electronics had appeared in this industry) Olivetti was the world's largest producer of calculating machines. By 1972 the company still held 37 per cent of the market for mechanical calculators, but only 3 per cent of the all-important new market for electronic machines. By 1980, following the change in methods of production designed to favour these electronic machines, Olivetti was a strong competitor in most of the major new markets. It led the world in the manufacture of accounting machines and systems and printing calculators; it was second in mini-computers for technical and scientific use and for both office and portable type-writers; and it was third largest for printing terminals and teleprinters, as well as being recognized as the greatest technological pioneer. None of this would have been possible without changes in organization and working methods.

The trade union view

Although the trade unions involved are in favour of changing organizations, they, like management, have found the process poses certain practical problems. For instance, just as some managers were apprehensive about delegating decisions to groups of workers, so were some full-time regional trade union officials. Usually the problem was found to be closely related to the extent of involvement of those concerned. Like management, their fears diminished as their practical experience grew. Also, like management, the unions found that employees welcomed the increased job satisfaction, pay and career prospects offered by the new methods.

However, valuable though this is, the trade unions are looking for more. The vital question for senior regional and national officials is how far are their wider political and social objectives being achieved. Opinions vary widely, as might be expected over an issue where assessment is so difficult and so subjective. Some officials felt that something useful had been achieved, particularly in terms of workers' control over day-to-day matters. This was felt to be especially true of what had been done at Olivetti, Italsider and Graziano where trade union officials seemed largely to trust the motives of the senior managers and the internal advisers involved.

Conversely, other officials saw the changes as 'a socio-psychological trick to get the workers to fight the trade unions' or to 'divert the unions from their interest in wider issues like investment'. Many regional officials feared a 'loss of control' by the unions as a result of the changes and 'an unacceptable integration of workers with management'. The controversy seemed to centre particularly on Fiat. This is perhaps not surprising. The company is the largest capitalist enterprise in the country – so large that in some years it contributes about 10 per cent of the country's GNP – and the trade unions in the Turin area (where Fiat employs huge numbers of people) are particularly well organized. A clash of views seems to be inevitable.

As the trade unions see it, the company's chief motive in introducing change, apart from wishing to exploit workers in an attempt to increase profits, is to undermine union power within the plants. In particular, the unions contend, managers are using new technology to further these aims. For instance they are said to be deliberately automating out 'the hot spots', jobs like welding and the marriage of body and power train where conflict in industrial relations is traditionally high. Group solidarity is being destroyed because workers on automatic processes (like Digitron) tend to be more isolated than those on assembly lines. Automation also allows the building of smaller factories, a move which, reinforced by an increase in the amount of work put out to non-unionised home workers, 'breaks up the large concentrations of labour where the unions can base their power'. The unions are by no means against automation. They recognize that it can and has improved working conditions enormously and they welcome this. They are simply against what they see as its 'misuse'.

The unions cite the abandonment of the experiment at Rivalta in island assembly as an illustration of management's true attitude: managers contend that the method proved uneconomic. In the unions' view, however, it could have been successful. The obstacle as they see it – probably with some realism – was that management was trying to 'solve operational problems with mathematical models. The only solution was to let the workers decide how to cope'. Continuing with the experiment would have obliged management to accept 'the greater autonomy of the working groups, and Fiat couldn't cope ideologically with this'.

But even though trade union officials have different views about the extent to which changes in work organization have helped them to achieve their social and political aims, they do not wish the new path to be abandoned; far from it. It seems that they are convinced that the issues over which they have chosen to fight capitalist managers are indeed the appropriate ones; disagreements with management about what is going on simply increase this conviction.

Overall assessment

Whilst we must be wary of transplanting solutions from one culture to another, we can learn by considering the approaches others have made to similar problems. Management in significant companies in the Italian metal industries, faced with pressures for change from customers, staff and highly organized, politically motivated trade unions, have been able to devise, negotiate and implement changes which have offered something to all parties concerned and have proved satisfactory to many. These are the factors which have played an important part in the achievement of such benefits:

(i) Management were convinced of the operational importance of responding to changing customer and staff needs.

(ii) Both managers and union officials felt that the problems which could result from resisting change would be greater than the problems involved in making changes: therefore both sides acted positively when difficulties arose, but without compromising their basic principles.

(iii) Employees were involved in various ways in determining the changes, in some cases directly, in others through steering groups, working parties and other forms of representation.

(iv) The crucial importance of the supervisor's role in the new way of working was recognized and suffcient training and support were given to enable supervisors to cope with the anxieties that their new role tended to arouse.

(v) The scope of collective bargaining at both national and local level encompasses changes in work organization. Thus both management and unions have a clear framework for discussion and for developing their own strategies; when changes lead to higher skills being required, higher pay can be negotiated.

(vi) In assessing progress both sides applied existing quantitative measures where possible, as well as trying to develop new ones. But they felt that it was neither possible nor desirable to rely exclusively on measurement, finding that they also had to rely on their judgement and the reactions of those involved in order to assess some of the most important outcomes.

In conclusion, the most significant lesson to emerge from the Italian experience is this: that it is not necessary to agree about aims in order to make progress. Management in the Italian metal working industries distrusts the unions' political motivation. The unions distrust what they see as management's preoccupation with profit and productivity. But neither side has allowed its distrust to stand in the way of coming to terms with the other, and the results have been useful to both.

6 The British Civil Service

1. Background

The British Civil Service is one of the largest employers of white-collar workers anywhere in the world. In 1971 when it employed over half a million clerical, executive and managerial staff, it embarked on a project designed to improve the satisfaction its employees derive from their jobs and the service they give to the public – a project which has since become one of the longest-running programmes of its kind in the world, and certainly one of the most radical. For these reasons I have chosen it as one of the case studies.

Before describing what has happened it is worth setting straight a few popular misconceptions about the function of managers in the Civil Service. While it is true, of course, that managers and staff in the Civil Service are not responsible for making a profit, it does not follow that managers in the private sector have nothing to learn from the experience of their public sector counterparts. The Civil Service is not composed of mandarins loftily considering policy options in Whitehall; those concerned with policy are very much in the minority. The majority of civil servants work in the bustle of local offices in direct contact with the public. They feel and behave just like people in other jobs. The main responsibility of their managers is to support and develop the capabilities of their staff, and to encourage them to do a good job for their customers, just as it is in the private sector.

Nor do civil servants have an easy time in industrial relations terms. While undoubtedly there are managers with greater problems in some parts of the private sector, those concerned with industrial relations in the Civil Service nowadays are provided with just as much challenge as any manager outside. The Civil Service trade unions' organization has been considerably strengthened. Trade unions are recognized for every job, and most civil servants are members of a union. Some 90 per cent are members either of the generally clerical Civil and Public Servants' Association (CPSA) or the generally executive Society of Civil and Public Servants (SCPS), and there are also unions covering specialist and technical jobs. The managers who negotiate are themselves being negotiated for, because trade union membership is high among managers too. The strikes of the late 1970s and early 1980s demonstrate the growing militancy of their members and the increased professionalism of their officials. These unions severally and together have become a more formidable force than most private sector managers of white-collar staff ever encounter.

A second misconception is that changing the way work is organized and improving job satisfaction is somehow simpler in the office than in the factory where jobs are characteristically 'tied to machines'. It is true that technology imposes constraints – and there is expensive technology in Civil Service offices as well as in private sector factories – but the responsibility of public accountability imposes constraints too. These can be every bit as burdensome as the constraints encountered in private industry. In fact while working with the Civil Service on this project I have often felt that if civil servants can create freedom to change for themselves then anyone can!

Finally there is the popular belief that civil servants are immune from the effects of customers' dissatisfaction. They are not. A statement like this often comes as something of a surprise to those outside the Civil Service. People working in the private sector, knowing that civil servants do not face the ultimate sanction of bankrupcty, underestimate the pressures on them. Customer dissatisfaction threatens the Civil Service just as it threatens the survival of any organization; the difference in the case of the Civil Service is that the issue is blurred.

Individual citizens are, after all, compelled to deal with certain parts of the Civil Service. We still have to pay our income tax, make our national insurance contributions and licence ourselves to drive whether we like the way the system treats us or not. Admittedly there are ways of avoiding the kind of frustrations we might encounter: for instance, while some people pay others to deal with income tax or VAT for them, others never get round to completing their forms. Where use of the system is not compulsory there are other ways out. For instance, some people going abroad on holiday choose to pay for health insurance arranged by their travel agent rather than get their local Social Security office to arrange it for them free. Some who can afford it choose to use their savings to see them through times of unemployment rather than run the risk of humiliation by claiming the unemployment benefit to which they are entitled.

But the fact that some people choose not to be customers and that others are only customers under compulsion does not mean that customers' dissatisfaction does not matter. There is always the possibility of political sanctions initiated in Parliament, and the Private Member's question and the letters of constituents to their MPs are still taken extremely seriously throughout the Civil Service hierarchy. The effect on civil servants of the political and public criticism encountered during the Conservative Thatcher administration of the early 1980s has indeed been marked, both in terms of depressing morale and increasing self-criticism.

A public sector organization in a democracy is in trouble if its customers are not satisfied with the way they are treated, even if this apparently saves the country money in the short term. Ultimately, as in the private sector, the customer is the boss. If the customer decides not to deal with an organization, that organization is in difficulties. It has to respond, or in the end it will be brought to a halt and the cost of an organization in the public sector coming to a halt is too high: not just financially in terms of the cost of misuse of the system, but socially and morally in terms of the undermining of respect for government and of threats to public order.

Most civil servants understand this and they are trying to respond. For example, the Department of Employment is endeavouring to make it clear to the unemployed that they are entitled to benefit and that they should claim and the Inland Revenue has set up and advertises special public enquiry offices. The Civil Service has to keep pace with the changing needs of its employees and its customers just like any other organization.

2. The problems faced

The problems which in 1971 compelled senior civil service managers to embark on this project were essentially similar to those which initiated change in the car industry and in the Italian metal working sector: the changing expectations of employees on the one hand and of customers on the other. As in the other case studies, this general phenomenon, which has had an impact on managers in all kinds of organizations all over the world, has taken its own particular form in accordance with the unique job the Civil Service has to do.

During the 1950s and 1960s the British people had enjoyed constantly rising living standards and a higher level of employment than at any time in living memory. At the same time the creation of the 'welfare state' had helped to relieve people of many of their burdens, both by providing direct aid to those who could not support themselves and by assuming fuller responsibility for such services as education and health care.

One result of this upsurge in affluence and security was to increase expectations. People who in the pre-war era might have been grateful simply to hold a steady job and to feed their families had come to take these things for granted and began to demand more from their government and from their jobs.

From their government people began to demand a greater range of support and assistance – a style of government which is more 'interventionist'. At the same time, encouraged by politicians and the mass media, they came to expect higher standards as well as a greater range of service. Efficiency was no longer enough. Courtesy and humanity came to be expected. People no longer saw themselves as supplicants with requests, but rather as customers with rights.

From their jobs people came to demand more than just a good, steady wage. Having experienced a longer and less didactic education than their parents, they became more inclined to look for work that interested them and gave them the opportunity to use their discretion and their skills. And this applied to civil servants as much as to any other group of employees.

In order to operate the 'welfare state' and to administer the ever-growing range of social policies enacted by successive governments the British Civil Service grew rapidly in the post-war years. Much of the increase in work was of a routine nature and its execution was made all the more mechanical by contemporary trends in the thinking of senior managers and politicians. To ensure uniform treatment of the public and the safeguarding of public funds administrative methods came to be based on rigid specification of tasks and strong central control. This trend was intensified by the later need for compatibility with computers and related systems. At the clerical levels many civil servants were doing essentially 'assembly line' jobs – without the assembly line.

This rise in the aspirations of staff for more stimulating work coincided, especially in the clerical grades, with a reduction in the stimulation that their work actually offered. At the same time a rise in the expectations of customers for a service which treated each of them individually coincided with a reduction in the responsiveness actually experienced. But because of their inflexibility administrative systems had become conducive neither to the morale of the staff nor to a humane and efficient service to the public.

When the Civil Service began its programme in 1971 this fact was far from clear, for it is notoriously difficult for the individual to understand changes in attitude of which he or she is a part. What officials were most aware of then was a sense of frustration amongst staff and a feeling that somehow a more flexible and responsive style of personnel management was called for.

Public dissatisfaction with the kind of service provided was also evident, but its seriousness and its link with the staff's dissatisfaction only began to become apparent as the pattern of project work unfolded. Even now, after more than a dozen years, this all important link is still proving elusive.

The Civil Service are not alone in finding it difficult to look at themselves from their customers' point of view. It is far more common to start from within, looking at the organization from its employees' point of view which is what the Civil Service did. In this they were influenced by the ideas of some contemporary behavioural scientists, particularly Maslow, McGregor and Herzberg, and by the experiences of other large organizations, like ICI and Shell in the UK, Philips in the Netherlands and AT&T in the USA, when trying to put these ideas into practice. What these organizations had been doing in essence was to redesign jobs, building in greater scope for individual achievement and recognition, more interesting and responsible work and more opportunity for personal development. This 'job enrichment' approach was adapted to form the basis of the early work in the Civil Service. It turned out to be just the starting point: it was an attempt to find a way into the problems which senior management felt they faced.

3. The changes made

Since it began, this work has, at one time or another, involved nearly every major department and some minor departments of central government. These include the Inland Revenue, the Department for

National Savings, the then Civil Service Department and the Treasury, the Department of Health and Social Security, the Ministry of Defence, the Departments of Environment and Transport, the Office of Population Censuses and Surveys, the Department of Employment, the Lord Chancellor's Department, Her Majesty's Stationery Office and the British Library. It has affected several thousand people from a wide range of levels and functions: clerical, executive and managerial as well as specialist, technical and professional; and a variety of establishments: local and regional offices, large clerical complexes, computer centres, headquarters policy divisions and research establishments.

Each department, indeed each location, that has taken part has done so for operational reasons of its own. All kinds of problem have been tackled, among which are low morale and high labour turnover; pressure of work and associated backlog; and those raised by the introduction of a new computer-based organization. Attempts have been made to improve work procedures, personnel management, the quality of service given to the public, and the effectiveness of joint consultation within the Civil Service. The precise changes made are, of course, tremendously varied because they were designed to meet so many different circumstances. But underlying all this diversity, the new ways of working do have certain common characteristics – and this despite the fact that in the early days they were largely proposed by professional advisers, while later they were devised entirely by civil servants themselves.

Although the environments have been very different the changes made have a good deal in common with those made in the car industry and in the Italian metal working sector. Here are some examples of the kind of changes that have been achieved so far.

Work procedures and organization

Work procedures have been changed in the direction of creating 'whole jobs' out of a number of previously fragmented tasks, giving people more opportunity to follow a piece of work through. Responsibility has been pulled down the organization towards the place where it most naturally fits: the level of the person actually doing the job. This has meant that people have more flexibility and more opportunity to take decisions according to local circumstances instead of uniformly imposed sets of rules. Not that the basic rules have ever been set aside; the Civil Service operates within a legally defined framework and this framework must always be respected.

In some cases increased scope for making decisions has gone hand in hand with increased responsibility for quality. People now carry out final checks on their own work rather than simply passing it up for examination. In other cases continuous two-way communication has started between people doing 'production' jobs, (like producing an assessment of supplementary benefit due), and those working in supporting jobs like 'quality control' and training. Many offices found that 'autonomous' and 'semi-autonomous' groups (although this was not the terminology used) offered the right kind of framework for enabling jobs and procedures to be redesigned.

In a hierarchy like the Civil Service such changes have widespread implications and require complementary readjustments, particularly in the role of management and in the role of the centre *vis-à-vis* the local level. As clerks in the lower grades became more responsible for quality and for more of the day-to-day operational decisions, their supervisors and managers moved towards a 'support' role. This meant they spent less of their time in checking and controlling staff and more in developing their subordinates and advising them on difficult matters which required a wider perspective and greater experience. To use the words of one manager, they became more like 'real managers' and less like 'supercheckers'. With this new relationship between levels it became natural too for managers to consult their staff more, to involve them in decisions and to keep them well informed.

Similarly, as responsibility moved down the organization it became less appropriate for those at the centre to issue orders. They had to learn to relax their previously rigid control, to consult local staff and management, to listen to their views before formulating policy and to accept that staff actually dealing with the public were in many ways the 'experts'.

In some projects the changes in procedures went further than in others. There is no uniform pattern but here are some concrete examples. The **Department for National Savings at Durham** took part in one of the early consultant-led projects. Initially it was very much a 'clerical factory'; clerical jobs were essentially of a fragmented, repetitive, flow-line type; work was measured, and individual daily outputs were recorded in an attempt to ensure the efficiency and quality of production. Supervisors were checkers; their work included relatively little management.

The system seemed on the surface to be efficient, but analysis showed that the flow was not as smooth as it looked. Concealed stocks of work built up on each section and the lack of communication between sections led to each blaming the others for delays. The statistics for each individual's output totally masked the actual performance of the line as a whole, but, at the same time, caused considerable stress to staff. The fragmented nature of operations greatly diminished people's sense of co-operative working towards the goal of serving the public – the feeling on which the efficiency and quality of production must ultimately be based.

The changes introduced aimed at creating this sense of purpose and at making the office less of a 'clerical factory'. In one section composite teams were formed, each dealing with some of the more interesting enquiry work as well as the routine processing of documents. In another section clerical staff who had previously performed nothing but isolated tasks in rotation were formed into groups handling the whole range of necessary work.

The priority system was altered to help eliminate bottlenecks. Supervisors were given experimentally the responsibility of co-ordinating the work of the line and because they were now beginning to manage, individual records of output could be abolished, a move intended both to reduce the psychological pressure on clerical staff and to increase their sense of responsibility.

The clerks and their managers at the **Driver and Vehicle Licensing Centre, Swansea,** used similar principles in redesigning for themselves the way they worked. For instance, those in the Vehicle Enquiry Unit (VEU), which deals with public enquiries about vehicle licences, decided to combine the previously separate jobs of taking telephone enquiries and following up the case in order to send a reply.

Similarly in the 'Clerical Drivers Branch' teams of clerical staff took on all stages of processing driving licence applications – opening the post, editing, coding, batching and balancing – tasks which had hiterto been carried out by three different sections, working in separate locations.

These changes in procedure and organization were complemented by various kinds of problem-solving and discussion groups which improved communication greatly and encouraged the development of a new and constructive relationship between clerical staff and their managers.

Clerical staff and managers in various local offices of the **Department of Health and Social Security** also reviewed aspects of their organization and procedures. At Swansea a new organization structure, based largely on the ideas of clerical staff and their supervisors, was introduced. The most important feature was that 'customer service groups' of clerks, led by their supervisor, should be responsible for complete aspects of service, like pensions and so on. Managers at a higher level withdrew from direct supervision and instead used their greater experience to advise the customer service groups on difficult technical and personnel matters. The clerical staff at the Wallsend office reorganized their Supplementary Benefit section into what were effectively autonomous working groups, some dealing with the assessment work itself and others with supportive work like training and quality control – and all this within existing resources.

Personnel management and training

Such changes in work procedure and organization went hand in hand with changes in personnel management. Since the early 1970s personnel management in the Civil Service as a whole has been in the process of transformation. The changes introduced in offices taking part in job satisfaction projects have aimed broadly in the same direction, but often starting earlier and going further than the more general trend and often, therefore, influencing it as a result.

For instance, the first job satisfaction project (in the Inland Revenue) saw the introduction of flexible working hours for the first time in the Civil Service. By 1975 such schemes had become relatively commonplace. Nonetheless the staff of the Wallsend Social Security office successfully devised a scheme which allowed far greater flexibility than the norm – and by far more participative methods than were usual – thereby demonstrating how much further the rest of the Civil Service could safely go.

Staff reporting has contined to be a subject of interest, with people examining the management level at which reports are officially required to be completed; the usefulness of the standard Civil Service form; and the extent of the openness with which the whole procedure is conducted. Some improvements have been introduced locally, but the uniformity of normal Civil Service practice has made it difficult for innovators to make headway. Nonetheless the experience of those who have taken part in job satisfaction projects has much to offer those responsible for deciding what normal practice should be.

There have been greater advances in the area of recruitment. Traditionally recruitment is a relatively centralized function in the Civil Service. By and large the local manager has to accept the staff that he is given. His needs and preferences are borne in mind to some extent, but they are not always given sufficient weight in the eyes of many local managers. Job satisfaction projects have frequently increased the influence of the local manager over staff recruitment and in some cases it has also been possible to involve in the selection process the supervisors who would actually have to work with the new recruits.

Training was the aspect of personnel management in which the need for change was greatest. Traditionally, training in the Civil Service, as in other organizations, concentrated on teaching people the technical information and skills needed to do their jobs. This will always be essential, however work is organized, whether by 'flow line' or 'autonomous group'. But as staff begin to work in groups and to have a voice in decisions, and as their managers become more concerned with staff development, skills of a different kind are needed as well as these technical skills. If the new ways of organizing work are to be efficient, then people at all levels need help to increase their ability to analyse problems and formulate solutions, and to bring out the best in their colleagues and their subordinates. This is the kind of help that the training devised on 'job satisfaction' projects aimed to provide.

This newer type of training was often devised by local staff and their managers to meet their own particular needs – another departure from the normal practice of the training expert carrying out this role. So the very process of developing the new method of training gave training specialists at regional and headquarters levels the opportunity to play a more supportive role, placing their expertise at the service of their internal customers. This in turn stimulated the training staff to review and improve the way they responded to their customers and organized their own work, notably in the DHSS.

Service to the public

Implicit in all these different changes in working procedures and organization and personnel management was the desire to improve service to the public. This is what actually gives civil servants their satisfaction, as each of the projects demonstrates. This desire for improving service was behind the complete reorganization of the DHSS, Swansea, into 'customer service' groups and the introduction of quality control sections at the DHSS at Wallsend and Wakefield. It was behind the amalgamation of the jobs of telephone and correspondence clerks at the DVLC, Swansea and so on.

But although civil servants are concerned to provide a good service, a considerable change of perspective is needed before they begin to look at the quality of service they provide explicitly from the customers' point of view. The process of helping them to do this can be slow and difficult. A bureaucratic hierarchy – and although the Civil Service is changing it is still essentially this – encourages people to look inwards rather than outwards. The dominant theme is the reduction of unpredictability and the strengthening of internal controls. Once people start looking outwards to the unpredictable customer (particularly in departments like the DHSS and the DE where the work load is essentially demand-led) the whole system is put at risk. This makes people anxious and so they try to avoid looking outwards, and civil servants are not alone in this, as many customers of firms in the private sector can testify.

Despite these difficulties progress is being made. At first only tentative moves were made, like the rudimentary survey of customers' attitudes to the way the public counter was arranged, carried out by clerks at the DHSS, Wakefield. But now innovation is more confident. Indeed, one of the explicit aims of a major project, the 'Local Office Project', which began in 1978, was to improve service to the public.

As part of this project, staff in South Wales in several Unemployment Benefit Offices in the **Department of Employment (DE)** between them have:

(i) designed and distributed simple leaflets and letters to explain office procedures to certain groups of claimants and to help them fill in claim forms correctly, as well as proposing simpler versions of official leaflets and forms, specially adapted for local circumstances;

(ii) pressed the Department's computer centre to improve those parts of computer-issued letters that claimants found incomprehensible;

(iii) visited local firms to ensure that redundant workers understood their entitlement to benefit instead of leaving it to the workers to come for advice;

(iv) put forward suggestions to improve arrangements at the public counter, in particular improving communication through the officially required screens;

(v) initiated exchange visits with other government departments who deal with the public in the same locality on the same work (the DHSS and other parts of the DE) with the aim of improving relationships and communication;

(vi) requested, as an adjunct to the normal course, a local training course designed to improve interviewing skills, and they helped to devise it (members of the public were actually invited to take part as 'interviewees', an initiative which greatly aided mutual understanding);

(vii) suggested and costed a mobile benefit office to visit isolated customers who could not easily visit them.

The staff of **Cardiff County Court in the Lord Chancellor's Department (LCD)** were also involved in the 'Local Office Project'. County Court staff have taken the initiative in improving relationships and mutual understanding with all their major users – solicitors, Citizens' Advice Bureaux and Matrimonial Service Officers and so on. This has enabled changes in the office's organization and procedures to be based on customers' views as well as those of staff and it has created personal links between Court staff and users which speed the flow of work. And it has helped create an outward-looking perspective which with the right encouragement should be of benefit to staff and public alike.

Joint consultation

There is in the Civil Service a long history of joint consultation through the Whitley system of committees involving management and trade unions, from national level down to regional and often local level. The trade unions were, therefore, always involved in the programme for improving job satisfaction, although in different ways at different times, as Section 4, 'How the changes were made', will describe. However, although joint consultation has a long history, it has not always had much substance. Consultation was characteristically somewhat formal and matters like work organization were generally excluded, not surprisingly as they were not regularly discussed with staff.

Project activity helped to change this. The increased involvement of staff in decisions about the way their office was run led to an increase in trade union involvement in operational matters generally beyond their influence. Also the canvassing of staff views that went along with project activity naturally put the representatives in closer touch with their members. Together these changes gave the trade unions a new and more important role in offices where projects had taken place.

In the early days this kind of change emerged as a useful by-product of project activity. It was not initially seen as one of its aims. However, as trade union interest in the work grew, it became explicit policy to foster such changes.

The 'Local Office Project' was the first project to include 'the improvement of arrangements for joint consultation' as one of its explicit aims. The offices in the Lord Chancellor's Department in the Department of Employment involved in this project were somewhat unusual in the Civil Service because they had not previously taken part in any local joint consultation. As part of the 'Local Office Project' they established local Whitley committees for the first time, not just for the duration of the project, but on a normal working basis. Thus employees, some for the first time, elected local trade union representatives and began to learn to use them. The representatives had to learn to do their new jobs; the managers had to learn to make the best use of this new resource. The information resulting from this experience should prove useful to those concerned with industrial relations, not just in the Civil Service, but also outside in industry and commerce. It is described in Section 5 below, 'What happened as a result'.

4. How the changes were made

These changes, significant though they are in Civil Service terms, may not look like much to the outsider. Indeed it is always easy to dismiss projects of this kind by reviewing the specific changes and concluding 'we work this way already. Our local managers recruit their own people and hold regular meetings with their shop stewards. Our employees are always on the look-out for changes in customer needs and so on. There is nothing we can learn from this project'. But this is to miss the point. The Civil Service 'job satisfaction' work has never aimed simply at changing procedures: it aims at changing attitudes. For this reason the way that the changes are made becomes particularly important. It is in these methods and in the roles played by junior staff, managers, trade union representatives and advisers that the real interest of Civil Service 'job satisfaction' work lies.

First it is worth saying something about the advisers, the 'Job Satisfaction Team' (JST) as they came to be called. They are a mixture of external consultants, contributing outside experience and a wider perspective, and civil servants who combine an understanding of the way the Civil Service operates with the personal qualities needed to look beyond established practice.

The 'Job Satisfaction Team' is part of the central personnel function (initially the Civil Service Department, now the Managerial and Personnel Office (MPO)). It is, therefore, available to all Government departments. However, it has become common practice for departments to complement JST advisers with their own people, who then receive on-the-job training from the JST in the skills of internal consultancy. The twin aims are to provide the JST with experience of the workings of the particular department and to provide the department with the nucleus of its own team of advisers should it decide to spread the project work more widely. There is the additional point that working as an internal adviser has also proved to be a powerful means of developing people as managers.

Over the years the advisers' task has altered considerably. Initially their methods were those of more or less classic job enrichment. On the hypothesis that satisfaction comes from doing challenging and responsible work, people's jobs were redesigned to make them more challenging and responsible. The advisers played a leading role in this redesign, often using 'brain-storming techniques' to take into account the views of managers and trade union representatives. The people doing the jobs were not involved, although no changes were introduced without their agreement.

Changes were introduced into 'experimental groups' and their effects carefully monitored over periods of about a year. Comparisons were made between results from these 'experimental groups' and carefully matched 'control groups' on 'before' and 'after' measures of both performance and job satisfaction. Performance was monitored by both existing and specially developed means, and job satisfaction by specially designed 'attitude surveys'. It was hoped that the enthusiasm generated by such experiments would act as a catalyst, encouraging managers in other offices and in other departments to pay more attention to the content of people's jobs. In this way it was anticipated that policies and procedures would be changed and that benefits would gradually permeate the Civil Service.

The early work produced many useful results, particularly in departments like the Inland Revenue and the Department of National Savings. There were improvements in performance, some of them dramatic, and people generally welcomed the changes and were unwilling to go back to the old ways of working. But these early projects were more significant for what they did not achieve. While some of the experimental changes were more widely implemented, others were not, even though apparently beneficial. The stumbling-block was that the hoped-for catalytic effect had not taken place. The projects had little practical effect on management attitudes, on departmental procedures and practices or even on how people felt about their jobs. Therefore they fell short of tackling the basic problem – or, put another way, the method did not deliver the hoped-for results.

With the benefit of hindsight the reasons for this failure are evident.

(i) The scope for enriching individual jobs was greatly restricted by the complex superstructure of regulations and controls. Because of the protected laboratory atmosphere of the early projects no attempt had been made to change this superstructure, nor to involve the more senior regional managers and policy-making staff at head-quarters who had a vested interest in preserving it. This tended to isolate the senior staff responsible for running departments and to prevent them from learning about the efforts of their own decisions. Among junior staff it tended to arouse expectations which it could not adequately fulfil because, ultimately, what was being attempted was insufficiently radical.

(ii) The changes introduced were largely devised by consultants and managers. Thus, while people generally welcomed the new pro-cedures, they did not respond with the degree of understanding and enthusiasm that could have been expected if the initiative for change had been their own.

(iii) Although the relevant trade unions were kept fully informed from the start, they were not fully involved. Thus, like management and junior staff, their understanding of the work was limited, and so, therefore, was the scope for learning from it. As a result their commit-ment was insufficiently aroused.

(iv) The problem had been approached the wrong way round,

starting by experimenting with job procedures instead of concentrating on their ultimate purpose – service to the customer. The direct relationship at local level between the civil servant and the public (or other customers) that they serve would have made the best starting point, but it was not given sufficient prominence and so the greatest potential source of satisfaction – providing a worthwhile service effectively – went largely untapped.

In the light of this experience the next phase of project work was planned with the following objectives:

(i) improving not only satisfaction for staff, but also service to the public and to internal customers;

(ii) giving staff at all levels the opportunity to devise and test for themselves the changes they identified as being necessary, thereby gaining their commitment and building on local experience of operational problems;

(iii) involving senior regional managers and policy specialists from headquarters so that local initiatives had a chance of flourishing;

(iv) involving the trade unions more fully so that they could give their members appropriate advice and support;

(v) altering the role of the advisers from that of devising the changes to be tested to that of helping the staff to do this for themselves.

The first significant project in which this approach was tried out began in the Department of Health and Social Security (DHSS) in 1973. Originally it was called 'the Long Range Study of Social Security Administration' but it became known as 'the New Model Office Project', or NMO. This project has proved to be something of a turning point in the development of the JST's approach and so it is described below in some detail.

The project originated in response to a number of problems which had developed in the DHSS's network of 750 local offices by 1972. Staff were under great pressure. On the one hand successive new legislation had complicated and fragmented their work, and restricted the previously close relationships they had enjoyed with colleagues and with their customers. The fact that local staff typically had to cope with 30,000 pages of codes and instructions (of which about a third required amendment in any one year) speaks volumes. On the other hand, while they were struggling to cope, claimants' unions and other pressure groups poured criticism, much of it bitter and personalized, upon them. Generally, of course, it was not the staff so much as the system. But the staff could not change the system.

The frustrations generated eventually erupted in industrial action in certain offices by the autumn of 1972. Senior departmental managers recognized the seriousness of the situation and, having introduced some sensible short-term measures to take care of the immediate situation, they decided to embark upon a long range study to identify and correct the underlying difficulties. What they called for was 'a radical and imaginative' reappraisal of the whole social security operation aiming to 'identify the requirements of a sound and sensitive local administration for the next two decades'.

It was envisaged that after a period of widespread consultation the broad outline of the new system would be worked out and tested in certain locations. Following a review of this practical experience the new system would then be more widely implemented. This approach fell at the first hurdle: it proved impossible to achieve a consensus view of the nature of the Department's problem, let alone of the means of tackling it. All that seemed to be shared was the quite understandable desire for a period of stability free from any more imposed change.

Discussion which followed between the JST and the DHSS unit responsible for the 'Long Range Study' led to the adoption of a quite different approach. This approach took into account the crucial lesson of earlier job satisfaction projects: people will not be committed to changes that others have devised. If the characteristics of a really sound and sensitive local administration were to be identified, the team had to start in the local offices, not at the centre. They had to find out how local people saw operational problems and they had to harness local experience in the search for ways of solving them.

There were no precedents for such a process; they had to think it out afresh. To start the process off, the staff and management of the local office in Swansea agreed to act as a 'laboratory' in which it would be possible for a mixed team of JST advisers and DHSS staff to find out whether it was practical to get local office people to define and solve their own work problem themselves and, if it were practical, to find out where it would lead. The ultimate aim, of course, was to find out how things should be, but understanding how things are done now had to be the first step. It seems that people only genuinely come to understand how things are done when they are free to change them and on this hypothesis, the joint JST/DHSS team secured quite unusual freedom for local staff to experiment.

Both management and the trade unions agreed that, statutory limitations apart, all the rules, constraints and joint agreements under which local offices normally operate would be formally waived for the period of this project. People were to have freedom to decide for themselves how they should work in order to provide a more personal and effective service to the public. For the Civil Service this was a remarkable departure – and a courageous one. This kind of freedom has since become an essential part of the JST's approach – with the all-important proviso (itself a lesson from the Swansea project) that anyone affected by a prospective change must agree to its being tried out before it is actually implemented.

The JST/DHSS team spent about nine months in the Swansea office. Their first priority was to get to know the clerks, managers and trade union representatives and to encourage them to think critically about the strengths and weaknesses of how they were working as a prelude to helping them to identify what changes they would like to try out. As a start the team interviewed every member of the office individually and confidentially. Since there were around 120 staff this was time-consuming, but it turned out to be crucial. In later projects the JST has tried to save time by interviewing fewer people, or carrying out group discussions instead: it has never been so effective. Some of the people not interviewed feel left out and some people will not speak up in a group. But above all it seems that the experience of working in a bureaucracy has undermined civil servants' self respect to the extent that many of them lack the confidence to formulate and put forward ideas for change. Only individual work can build up this confidence. Therefore the individual interviews at the start of a project have become an important part of the JST approach.

Out of these interviews came a picture of how the Swansea clerks and managers saw their Department and the service it provided. The team fed this picture back to clerks and managers and brought people together in groups for discussions on some of the issues raised; in turn these discussions yielded further information. This process of feedback and further discussion has also become common JST practice. The whole process demonstrated conclusively not only that people could think critically about their work, but also that they could clearly define the operational problems they faced and that they were quite capable of developing constructive solutions.

The next step was to get the clerks and their managers to use their insight to introduce practical improvements. This proved to be more difficult. People at all levels lacked experience of reconciling different points of view, but above all they lacked the confidence to translate ideas into reality. Frustration grew as time seemed to be 'wasting' away with no tangible results to show for all the effort. Pressure for 'something to happen' increased from those in headquarters at the DHSS and from the then Civil Service Department who wanted to see where the new approach would lead. The JST were faced with two apparent alternatives: one, to concentrate on developing the confidence of Swansea's management team so that they could themselves devise and test new ways of working and encourage the rest of the office to do the same; the other, to propose a specific change in organization which would break through the frustration and stimulate further development.

Rightly or wrongly the JST felt that the former would be too time-consuming in view of the mounting pressure for something to happen. Therefore, with the agreement of Swansea clerical staff and management, they proposed in broad outline a new organization based on ideas which had been put forward by clerical staff and supervisors. The basic concept (as described above in Section 3, 'The changes made') was that 'customer service groups' of clerks led by their supervisors should be responsible for complete aspects of service to the public, such as pensions, supplementary benefit and so on. Senior managers would provide advice and support to those groups, instead of controlling them directly in the traditional way. This initiative was, at the time, welcomed by the Swansea clerks and managers, who then set about working out the practical details: deciding for themselves exactly which customer service groups there should be; who would work in which group; how the office layout should be altered; how any necessary training should be handled and so on. Once implemented the new structure was refined in the light of practical experience.

In terms of performance and in the views of the clerks and even of the public there was much to justify this new way of working. But the process had brought evident problems for the management team – and here there were important lessons for the JST. Looking back it seems that despite their enthusiastic acceptance of the JST's proposal at the time, managers found that the new organization had catapulted them into a role which they were not ready to fill. To a lesser extent some of the supervisors and clerks met the same difficulty. There were two lesson in this. First, people need help, in the form of special training, sympathetic support and so on, before they can play roles which, in many ways, conflict with their previous experience. Obvious perhaps, looking back, but at the time of the JST's proposal managers were enthusiastic about going ahead.

The second lesson for the JST advisers, and one that has been reinforced by their experience in other projects, was that if a change is to be successful, those involved must themselves work through all the stages necessary to implement and test it. That the initial ideas are theirs is not enough. Without going through the whole, sometimes painfully slow, process of translating ideas into something practical and testable they will not be fully committed to making change work. Nor will they gain much understanding of the way that their organization operates. Their commitment is vital, but just as important is their understanding. It is this understanding and the ability to translate it into a continuous process of tested improvement that are the foundation of the 'sound and sensitive' organization that the DHSS and the then CSD were seeking. Or, in terms of the JST's approach, the 'means' is the end.

But all this was not so clear at the time. What was clear was that the Swansea managers and, to a lesser extent, some of the clerks and their supervisors, had been taken too far too fast and, quite understandably, they hankered after slipping back into more comfortable traditional authoritarian roles. There were other related problems, which reinforced the lessons being learnt by the JST. The freedom from customary constraints so necessary to stimulate experimentation at Swansea made the Swansea managers unlike their counterparts in other offices. This tended to isolate them and this isolation in turn undermined the experiment.

It isolated them too from senior managers and specialists in the Cardiff regional office who might otherwise have provided advice and support. The Cardiff people, well informed, but unable to control what was going on at Swansea, became understandably anxious. Their anxiety began in turn to undermine further the efforts of the Swansea people.

On the trade union side the pattern was similar. Local representatives were cut off from the advice and support of regional and national officials who, largely because they felt they could no longer exercise their traditional control, began in turn to lose sympathy for local experimentation. These lessons were not immediately apparent. They began to emerge slowly as experience elsewhere began to re-inforce them.

However, despite these difficulties, the Swansea project was rightly regarded as a success. The aims had been to begin to establish a clearer picture of the strengths and weaknesses of the DHSS's organization and to work out how to build upon its strengths and to do something about its weaknesses. As well as helping the DHSS to do this, the aim of the JST was to discover what happens when advisers help civil servants to improve for themselves the way they work.

There was no doubt that the nine months spent at Swansea had provided abundant source of such evidence. To take this process further, both the DHSS and the JST decided to move the experiment on to further locations. This time the units were to be the Regional Offices to whom the local offices reported, rather than single local offices, although the local level was again to be the initial level of experimentation. Northern Region (Wallsend office) and York and Humberside Region (Wakefield office) agreed to take part. Work began early in 1975.

The process was to be essentially similar to that used in Swansea in that clerks and managers in the new locations were to be free to look critically at the way they worked and to devise and try out potential improvements. But this time the office was not to be so isolated. Regional and headquarters officials and trade union representatives were to be more fully informed. They were also to be drawn into the local process of analysis and improvement so that they too would begin to learn and to experiment for themselves.

This meant limiting the local people's freedom to experiment. It was agreed that no change could be introduced, even experimentally, without the acceptance of all those affected by it, including local, regional and headquarters staff and trade union representatives. This was more realistic than the total freedom granted at Swansea. The Swansea freedom had in fact been more apparent than real. In prac-tice the agreement of regional and headquarters managers and trade union representatives to experiment was essential if local people were to be supported and local initiative to flourish. In the event making it obligatory to secure this agreement did not constrain local initiative greatly. Such was the prevailing lack of confidence that the problem was to get people to use the freedoms that were normally available to all DHSS staff, but not generally taken up.

Sensible though this may sound in theory, it proved to be difficult in practice. Inevitably there were differences of opinion about who was affected by any particular change. For instance, people at Wallsend could not understand why regional managers refused to agree to a change in the hours that the local office was open to the public. From Wallsend's point of view the proposed new hours would enable them to provide a better service to the Wallsend public. As far as they were concerned 'it was nobody else's business'. The anxiety at regional level was that, sensible though such a change might be locally, it might become a precedent with widespread political implications.

There were parallels on the trade union side. For example, local clerks wished to introduce special part-time arrangements to attract back to the office experienced women who had been forced by family responsibilities to give up full-time work. Union officials, however, felt that this cut across wider policies that they were pursuing nationally and so discouraged local people from going ahead. Even within Wallsend and Wakefield offices there were examples of the same problem. Changes were introduced by single sections within the offices without discussion beyond those sections, simply because their understanding of the flow of work in the office was so limited that they did not realize other sections would be affected.

Inevitably there were hold-ups, frustrations and disappointments, but it was only through drawing all levels of the Department – trade union as well as management – into the process that all levels could begin to understand the way they were working and so begin to initiate the radical improvements that the Department was seeking.

After about nine months of intense activity at local level, followed by further work by the JST with people at regional and headquarters level, it was decided to consolidate by crystallizing what had been learned so far and deciding how best to take the process further. The next question was who would carry out this review and how would it be done. The traditional Civil Service method would have been to hand the task over to an 'independent working party', probably composed of managers and specialists, and possibly also with a contribution from the trade unions. But this method did not meet the needs of the Long Range Study. It was not an 'independent' view that was necessary, but rather the views of those who had been through the change process. Only they had had the opportunity to look critically at normal practices because only they had been encouraged to change them. To give future developments a chance of success, it was also essential to include the views of senior departmental managers and trade unionists.

What followed took both the DHSS and the JST an important step further because it demonstrated that a viable process of diagnosis and change had been set in train: a process which, because it was based on the insights and efforts of ordinary civil servants, could place the DHSS (and therefore other government departments) on a far more secure footing than anything which was purely derived from outside expertise. So, the high-level group responsible for steering the project asked both the Northern Region and the Yorks and Humberside Region to hold conferences. Their purpose was to:

(i) clarify what had been learnt to date both about the nature of the DHSS's problems and the JST's approach;

(ii) make proposals about how what had been learnt could be applied.

It was left to the regions to decide how to proceed. Both opted to let those who had been involved speak for themselves. At Wallsend and Wakefield clerks, managers and trade union representatives organized discussions resulting in papers which stated their separate views. Similar papers were prepared in both the regional offices in Newcastle and Leeds. The papers formed the basis of a week-long conference in each region in which all levels of clerks, managers and trade union representatives thrashed out their differences through stormy, though constructive discussion. Out of the conferences came a concise picture of the Department's normal way of working, as seen through the eyes of clerks, managers and trade union representatives, and although the people in the two regions had tried out different ways of changing the normal picture, they were essentially in agreement as to what they had found.

They saw a rigid system in which, all too often, procedures over-emphasized uniformity at the expense of local discretion and responsive public service; a contradictory style of management, in theory aiming at participation and accountability, but in practice often hierarchical and authoritarian. Thus, given responsibility without sufficient opportunity to exercise it, clerks and managers had come to feel frustrated and vulnerable, and their initiative had been blunted.

The people in the two project regions concluded that this could be changed; indeed it had been changed in the local offices and it was in the process of being changed in their regions. What they proposed was simply that the process of analysis, change and review be continued locally; that it be intensified regionally; and that it be extended so that a reciprocal process took place at headquarters. In particular they wished for the specialists at headquarters and senior departmental managers to move away from their traditional roles of prescription and control towards those of advice and support; this would be both consistent with the local initiatives taking place and would encourage them to go further.

These conferences held another valuable lesson for the JST: it was that just as the process of problem identification and solution could best be carried out by the people involved, so could the evaluation of that process. Indeed when the aim of the project was to learn – and it was becoming increasingly clear that this must be the ultimate aim of all the JST's work – this was the only appropriate way of evaluating. This led to changes in the team's approach to evaluation away from the attitude surveys and performance indicators of the early 'job enrichment' days. Performance is still carefully monitored, but solely to ensure that service to the public is not suffering as a result of project work.

The team has simply begun to ask, using various techniques, what people have learned both about their normal way of working and about the team's approach. For instance, at the licensing department, Swansea, individual, confidential interviews were held with all staff involved in the initial work. In other projects there have been group discussions, and in others people have prepared summary papers as the basis for discussions.

Clear though it was, the way ahead in the DHSS was not smooth. There was an understandable reluctance on the part of some senior people at headquarters to expose themselves to the same strains that they had seen local and regional people go through because, however rewarding, this process can at times be immensely stressful. On top of this, there were perfectly rational reasons for proceeding slowly.

But proceed the DHSS did, after a time lag and without formally relating its progress to the conclusions of the conferences or to the Long Range Study as such. What seems to be taking place now is, in fact, the transformation that the Department has been looking for. Slow, perhaps, and patchy; but such a pace is inevitable given the size of the operation and the complexity and political sensitivity of its task.

In 1977 at the time of the evaluation conferences the chief operational constraint on proceeding immediately along the lines proposed by local and regional people was the attitude of the trade unions and in this problem lay the most important lesson for the JST.

The people at Swansea had demonstrated that local office clerks could handle the project process. The Northern and the Yorks and Humberside regional phase demonstrated that local and regional managers could also be successfully involved; and even that some progress could be made at headquarters. What was missing was trade union commitment. Trade union fears were basically of three kinds. First, some representatives had political objections. Like some trade unionists outside the Civil Service, they felt that if you oppose a system you should do nothing to help it survive. By forging better relationships between junior staff and management the project was helping the system to survive. Although only a minority of representatives held these views, they proved to be influential at crucial times, particularly in using large block votes at the annual conference of one union to secure the withdrawal of that union's support of the project.

Secondly, there were more traditional objections. Some representatives believed that the balance of tangible benefit was loaded heavily towards management, rather than towards the junior staff who had taken on greater responsibilities with no compensatory increase in pay.

Thirdly, there were concerns very similar to those felt by management. Like many people involved in fundamental change, trade union officials had found it threatening as well as exciting. Initially they were interested in what might be achieved for their members. Then, as local experimentation began to bite, they became uncomfortably aware that the changes had implications for them as well as for management. Like management, they felt that their traditional role was being eroded and they feared the consequences for trade unionism, just as managers feared the consequences for management.

One element in this was a misunderstanding of what had been going on. However, it was not just a matter of understanding. The situation was not without risk to the Civil Service's Whitley system of joint consultation. As it turned out, joint consultation in general and the role of the local trade union representative in particular was strengthened by the project. But this might not have been the case. The significant point was that the unions felt their interests were inadequately safeguarded. To encourage experimentation they had allowed staff freedom from existing joint agreements and in addition departmental and regional union officials did not insist on knowing what was being implemented locally.

On management's side, by contrast, local freedom to experiment was in practice restricted by the need to inform regional and head-quarters managers and, where appropriate, to secure their permission. Thus senior managers not only knew what was going on, they could also stop it. The trade unions did not have the safeguard of this power of veto and so they felt more vulnerable.

The Swansea phase of the DHSS project demonstrated that progress depends upon managers at all levels being fully involved as well as informed in order to protect their interests. The Northern and the Yorks and Humberside regional phase demonstrated that this was equally true of the trade unions at regional and central levels. This lesson was learnt too late to allow the logical extension of the DHSS work, following the regional evaluation conferences. But, reinforced as it has been by JST experience in other departments, it is a lesson which has proved to be immensely valuable.

What it led to was the signing in the summer of 1977 of a national agreement ratified by all the Civil Service trade unions, in effect giving the unions joint control with management over the work of the JST. Under this agreement a jointly composed National Steering Group was set up to guide the JST's work: it was to establish priorities, decide about resources and consider the implications of the work both for personnel management policies generally and for the strengthening of joint consultation through the Whitley system. This agreement, despite the inevitable difficulties for management and the unions of learning how to work together in this way, is proving to be a far more satisfactory framework for the JST's work. It has made possible projects which explicitly aim to improve joint consultation, of which the 'Local Office Project' described above was the first example. (The changes made in local arrangements are described in Section 3 above and their effects in Section 5 below, 'What happened as a result'.)

This project is important because in its emphasis on improving joint consultation it ushered in another new phase in the development of the JST's methodology. But it is also important because it introduced another element in their approach: the improvement of service to the public as an explicit aim. In planning the 'Local Office Project' the JST envisaged co-operative working between the local offices of a number of government departments to improve service to the community. A degree of public involvement was also anticipated, but this is not how things turned out. Useful changes were made, but the outward-looking perspective did not develop to the hoped-for extent. Up to a point this was inevitable because it proved to be impossible to secure the participation of departments which provided related services to the same customers. Two departments did take part – a County Court and several Unemployment Benefit Offices in the Department of Employment – but their work is hardly related at all. Also it proved impossible to set up the project within one community (in the event the County Court was in Cardiff and the Unemployment Benefit offices in Newport, Pontypool and Cwmbran).

The very fact that the project had to be set up in a way which was only second best indicates the real problem: the Civil Service as a whole was not at that stage ready to look sufficiently outwards to its customers. These issues are not now so novel and it is possible that another Local Office Project designed along the lines originally envisaged will be able to take place. Such a project would be the logical next step in the development of the JST's approach. It would enable the Civil Service to learn more about how to provide a responsive and efficient service to its customers as well as a satisfying working life to its staff in a way which has not so far been available to them.

Since 1971 when the work began there has been tremendous progress. A series of job enrichment projects have become a long term, participative organization development project on a massive scale, capable ultimately of improving the working lives of the many thousands of people who work for the Civil Service and the quality of life of the 56 million people whom they serve. The junior staff and their managers and their trade unions are now all participating, patchily and always with individual exceptions, but the framework for involving them is there and it has been shown to work. What is now needed is to get the public involved too. In my view the full potential of this kind of approach can only be realized when the organization using it looks outwards to the extent of actually seeking the involvement of its customers.

Before describing what happened as a result of applying the JST's approach it is worth pausing to summarize its chief elements.

(i) The aim is to set in train a continuous process in which civil servants and their trade unions analyse the problems they encounter in their working lives and develop, implement and test solutions. What is learnt thereby can then be more widely applied both by management and by the trade unions.

(ii) All civil servants and trade union officials affected by this process must be involved in it. The ideas for change must be theirs and they must themselves take the process from initial proposal through implementation to test and review.

(iii) The evaluation of what is learnt through this process must likewise be carried out by all those, junior staff, managers and trade union officials, who have taken part in it.

(iv) Internal and external advisers must work with junior staff, managers and trade union officials, encouraging them to make a start; supporting them while they learn to look critically at what they do; helping them to reconcile different opinions as they progress from initial idea through to evaluating the effects of implemented changes. Confidential individual interviews are important in building the confidence necessary to get this process off the ground. Information thus gathered about how people see the strengths and weakness of current operations can then be fed back to working groups. From this information and the resultant discussion junior staff, managers and trade union representatives can begin to determine their priorities. Ultimately the advisers must 'work themselves out of a job'.

(v) The involvement of the customer both in deciding what needs to be done and in its evaluation is important too. But actual customer participation is as yet at an early stage.

5. What happened as a result

It remains to describe what has happened as a result of adopting this approach, remembering what the Civil Service has been seeking: the characteristics of an organization which will provide both a responsive, efficient service to its customers and a satisfying working life to its employees. What seems to have happened is that the Civil Service is beginning to regenerate itself. From being an organization in which everything is determined and controlled from the top it is becoming one in which those in touch with the customer have much more say about how things should be done.

Project activity is altering the way offices function so that:

(i) People decide how best to do their jobs, bearing in mind genuine needs for uniformity.

(ii) People look critically at the way they work and feel that it is worth putting forward ideas for improvement.

(iii) People's ability to come up with constructive ideas is constantly being developed, both by training and by learning from experience.

(iv) Managers recognize that the people doing the job are the experts and encourage and enable them to do it in the best possible way.

(v) People's ability to put their ideas into practice is deliberately developed by training and by management support.

(vi) Managers and staff monitor their effectiveness constantly, primarily from the customers' point of view.

(vii) Those at headquarters let people know what the end product of their work should be, while leaving them free to decide the means (bearing in mind, legal requirements and genuine needs for uniformity). They then provide the help necessary to enable people at local level to do their jobs well and ensure that the policy advice that senior officials give to Ministers reflects accurately what goes on locally.

(viii) Trade union representatives play a full part in the life of these regenerated offices. As well as independently representing their members' interest in working conditions, they are involved in decisions about the way work should be done. 'Industrial relations' thus have real substance.

Such offices are not just a twinkle in the eye of an outside adviser; they are actually coming into being at Wallsend and Wakefield, Newport, Cardiff and Swansea, Southampton, Bath, Sidcup and elsewhere. The lessons learnt through project experience are being fed into policies made at headquarters and thus they are slowly, but steadily, beginning to permeate.

It is important to recognize that we do not have to wait for every office to have its own 'job satisfaction project' before the Civil Service can become both responsive to customers' needs and a satisfying place to work. This would take far too long. In any case, it would not be the most effective means because the potential for change at local level will always be limited, as much of it has been so far, until the centre also changes the way it operates. Nor can diffusion be a matter of introducing successful project changes into other offices. They may not suit all other local circumstances. More important, they would be seen as another round of imposed changes by other staff and would thus dull rather than stimulate their initiative. Here are some examples of the lessons now influencing central policy.

Job satisfaction

Job satisfaction comes from doing a worthwhile job well. The Civil Service is not short of worthwhile jobs; nor is it short of people who want to do them well. It is, therefore, a waste of time for people at the centre in personnel to look for techniques of 'improving staff morale'. They should simply help promote the circumstances in which people can do their jobs well.

Training

As well as being technically competent, people need to learn how to work together effectively. Central and departmental training colleges are now providing training of this sort, particularly to managers who must in turn provide this support to their subordinates.

Staff reporting

The most important function of staff reporting is to encourage the improvement of people's effectiveness, by identifying strengths which can be built upon and weaknesses where help is required. Traditionally restrictive reporting procedures are being amended to encourage openness and freedom to discuss.

Codes and instructions

Detailed, uniform, codes of instructions issued by those at head-quarters are unlikely to take full account of local circumstances. Thus, as well as blunting initiative, they can actually inhibit the high standard of service that they were designed to ensure. Departments like the DHSS are moving away from mandatory instructions, towards codes which, apart from specifying legal requirements and other vital information, leave local people the discretion they need to do their job well.

Premises and office layout

Central purchasing may secure reasonable prices, but differing local circumstances can render 'standard issue' equipment and layout ineffective and expensive. Progress is slow, but some officials responsible for premises are now offering the people who work in an office more say in how it is laid out and equipped, and some of these local staff are beginning to consult their customers.

Technology

The full potential of new technology can only be realized if staff are involved in decisions about its use. The Central Communications and Telecommunications Agency, the body responsible for new technology in the Civil Service, now has this firmly in mind.

Conditions of employment

The successful introduction of flexible working hours indicates that more flexible conditions of employment can be beneficial. For instance, various forms of part-time employment, job sharing and flexible annual working hours could all enable staff to balance their lives more satisfactorily as well as provide more responsive service. But as yet neither management nor the trade unions are about to experiment with such options.

Industrial relations

Active local trade union representatives can be an asset to management, providing an additional reflection of staff views on important issues. Such representatives can also be an asset to the unions, advancing members' interests far more than can national officials alone. But local industrial relations can only be given useful life if both senior managers and senior trade union officials allow their local people to deal with pertinent issues and provide the training and support they need to enable them to do this well. Some departments, like the Department of Employment, are relaxing their centralized grip and providing training in industrial relations for their managers. And the trade unions are beginning to take equivalent measures.

Control mechanisms

Traditional control mechanisms designed to ensure 'public accountability' have unintended consequences which can actually conflict with the public interest. For instance, rigid security procedures and complicated financial rules can become rituals, stifling common sense and local initiative – crucial factors in fraud prevention. Over-emphasis on checking can weaken a supervisor's authority, eating up his time on complex checks and preventing him from identifying and solving the problems which cause poor performance. Central control of staff numbers, equipment and working methods can drive local managers to 'play the system' to ensure that they get what they need. Emphasis on conformity and caution can cause excessive defensiveness. This leads to delays which in turn can contribute to over-manning. It is very hard to break through the mentality induced by such control mechanisms. A senior manager in the private sector may say, 'give the local managers budgets, train them properly and let them get on with it. Then you can really hold them accountable for how they perform.' The Civil Service is still some way from feeling able to do this. Senior officials fear that without traditional control mechanisms the public will suffer. It may suffer now, but 'better the devil you know' – particularly in an organization accustomed for so long to looking inwards and servicing its own system, rather than looking outwards and serving its customers.

Even in this most difficult area there is movement; these lessons are all the time reinforced by project activity and with the current popular emphasis on improving the cost effectiveness of the Civil Service a breakthrough ought not to be far away.

Two questions remain after describing what happened as a result of applying the 'job satisfaction' approach. First, what was it like for the people who took part in the projects which have stimulated regeneration? Second, what happened to the performance of their offices while they were so engaged; or, put another way, can we, the public, afford this kind of activity in our Civil Service?

The people who have taken part feel very much like other people – in the car industry, the Italian metal working sector or wherever – who have gone through this kind of experience. Fundamental change is exciting; it is exhilarating to see the system move forward because of your efforts; it is refreshing to earn the right to use your common sense and your experience; and it is a relief to be able to respond directly to people who come into your office needing your help. On the other hand it is frustrating and dispiriting when managers at higher levels are not prepared to respond. It can also be disorientating to find you are free to change the rules which have ordered your world and awesome to face up to responsibility for your own actions.

For some managers it is hard to learn to trust their subordinates and to overcome the fear that more scope for subordinates will mean less scope for managers. Will management 'lose control' and the customer suffer as a result?

All this can be worrying for trade union representatives whose job it is to protect the interests of their members. Will everything that the trade unions have been fighting for be thrown away by a handful of local people who do not understand all the ins and outs of the wider issues?

For the advisers too it is an exhausting, though satisfying responsibility. Their role is often compared to that of a chemical 'catalyst' – an accurate comparison in that chemical catalysts facilitate change, but inaccurate in that chemical catalysts do not themselves undergo change. It is not possible to do this work well without yourself being affected by it.

However, despite the anxieties and frustrations – and these should not be underestimated – the great majority of junior staff, managers and trade union representatives who have been involved feel that these projects are well worthwhile. In almost all cases the co-operative way of working they have stimulated has lived on after the end of the so-called 'project phase' and the withdrawal of the advisers' support. It has survived what are sometimes quite determined efforts by managers and trade union officials outside the offices to stifle it and 'bring things back into line'. It has also survived in one locality the death of a wise and able office manager whose efforts had done so much to create it – and to whom that survival is indeed a fitting memorial.

The second question was what happened to performance as a result of civil servants engaging in this kind of project activity? Judged by all normal standards there is no reason to suppose that accuracy and throughput have suffered. In some cases they have improved dramatically. In all cases people continued to do their 'normal work' during the time-consuming initial phase when what would later become 'the new way of working' was being established. This does not indicate spare capacity in the system so much as a determined effort by staff and managers. No extra allowances were made above what was usually available.

Quality is a more difficult matter. Normal measures do not always allow sufficiently sensitive assessment of what is a complex mixture of intangibles. Where reasonable measures do exist, they indicate that nothing has suffered and indeed some improvements are evident. But essentially the assessment of quality remains a matter of judgement. In many cases it is management's view that quality has improved, as might be expected when people begin to look deliberately at their customers' needs and to acquire the freedom to respond.

What is needed to complete the picture is the view of the customers themselves. Projects have often led to a reduction in customer complaints, but this aside, there is a great shortage of information. Perhaps we can look forward to the time when 'local user groups' will work with joint management–trade union bodies to monitor quality of service at local level, but such days are not yet with us.

So, can the public really afford this activity in the Civil Service? The answer is certainly that we can. Indeed it might be more appropriate to ask how we, the public, can encourage this process of change so that we continue to help promote the creation of the responsive cost-effective Civil Service that we need. How can we afford not to?

PART III

Working better

7 Some practical ideas for improving the way people work

1. Introduction

The previous part of this book describes what some organizations have done to improve the quality of what they offer to their customers and to their employees. These organizations operate in different countries with different histories and different cultures. They come from both private and public sectors and provide a variety of products and services. They employ people of all sorts in their factories and offices, and the abilities, experience and perspectives of their managers – and their trade union representatives – vary considerably. None of them have applied any particular theory or used any particular technique. They have all proceeded pragmatically, doing whatever they felt would be most effective in their own situation.

As a result they have made changes of different kinds and they have gone about their projects in varying ways. Some have been more radical than others, as the wide variety of job cycle times and working patterns in the car industry demonstrates. Some have involved their workforce more than others. Compare, for instance, Italsider's efforts to train nine hundred workers so that they could take part in planning their new steel-making facility with the less ambitious policies of others who involve employees mainly through works councils and trade unions.

Yet, despite all these differences in what they have done and how far they have gone, the experiences of people in these organizations have a good deal in common. They share these experiences too with people in all kinds of other organizations; in factories, offices and public sector organizations in Australia and India, in the Civil Service in the USA, in factories in Israeli kibbutzim, in insurance companies in Sweden, in manufacturing and commercial organizations in the UK and so on. Moreover, advisers with different backgrounds and expertise, from social scientists to ergonomists and engineers, are beginning to find common ground where previously there was little.

Out of these common experiences are beginning to emerge new ideas about how to help organizations not just to survive, but also to work better. These new ideas are quite different from those which tended to guide such efforts in the past and they are far more appropriate to today's unpredictable world. They suggest quite different answers to the practical questions that people have in mind when considering what to do to improve performance.

This concluding part of the book draws together some of these new ideas and the practical answers they suggest to people's questions. But first, some words of warning. These ideas should not be seen as a universal panacea for introducing change successfully for there is no such thing. The crucial point about the process of change of the sort being undertaken by organizations like those in the case studies is that success is a matter of what you learn from experience and of how effectively you apply what you have learned as a part of normal operations, not just for the duration of some 'project phase'. All this takes time and effort. It means that an organization seeking the benefits that this kind of process of change can undoubtedly bring must be prepared to put in the time and effort to initiate its own experiences and to learn from them. But while there is no substitute for working things through like this, it is always possible to be helped along the way by looking at the experiences of others; an examination of what they have done can help you to find answers to some of the questions with which you may be presented.

2. Some basic questions and their answers

When people are considering the introduction of a programme to improve the way their organization works they often find they are looking for the answers to question like these:

At what should we be aiming?
What should we think of changing?
How should we go about it?
How do we know if we are on the right track?
What sort of help might we need and where can we get it?

These are some of the questions. The experience of people in organizations like those in the case studies suggests some of the answers, and these answers are discussed below.

At what should we be aiming?

Organizations wishing to thrive in today's rapidly changing world should not aim at setting up any sort of rigid structure. A rigid structure is designed to operate in a given set of circumstances, but today's circumstances are essentially unpredictable. Therefore organizations should aim at setting in motion a continuous process of identifying needs and responding to them. This means, for instance, that if your customers stop wanting mechanical business machines and start wanting electronic ones then you should be ready to modify your manufacturing procedures, the jobs of your production workers and their supervisors, your training, your control system and to provide these products more quickly and economically than your competitors.

In the public service it means that if your customers start insisting on being treated like people as well as receiving the right social security benefit at the right time, then you should be in a position to cater for their needs.

Achieving this sort of flexibility depends on your workforce using their initiative and know-how to the full. Telling them to do this is ineffective, even irrelevant; so is trying to motivate them to do it with money. What you need to do is to aim to provide the kind of working experience that encourages and enables them to do it. If people's jobs give them scope to use their initiative and know-how, and if their managers encourage and help them to do so, then they will tend to work intelligently, willingly, even enthusiastically. They will take pride in doing a good job and, as well as finding satisfaction, they will try whole-heartedly to give it.

What should we think of changing?

To achieve a flexible, responsive organization you must be prepared to change whatever you find needs to be changed. Potentially this includes anything and everything, from tangibles like technology, jobs, systems for grading and payment, and working conditions, to intangibles, like style or atmosphere, perspectives, power structures and relationships. It does not mean, however, that everything must change, simply that when people feel they can change things for the better then they should be free to try; and when the consolidation of improvements in one part of the organization depends on complementary changes in another part then people should be encouraged to respond. Nor does it mean that things must change all at once: they should be changed gradually, thoughtfully and at a pace with which people and production requirements can cope.

Changing the nature of the jobs that people do is likely to be particularly important. For instance we have seen from the case studies how in factories and offices alike responsibility has been passed downwards. People have been given more scope to take decisions and more opportunity to use and develop their skills. They have become the masters rather than the servants of technology. The isolation which comes with a job on an assembly-line has given way to working in teams with all their enhanced potential for variety of task and increase in social contact. The jobs of supervisors and managers have been changed too, offering them more scope to use their broader vision and requiring them to place more emphasis on developing their subordinates than on controlling them.

The scope for changing jobs and the benefits from it are likely to be greatest when technology does not act as a constraint either where expensive, fixed technology is not a prominent feature of the production system (as in most of the British Civil Service, for instance) or where new technology and new working methods are designed jointly (as in the car manufacturing companies and in Italsider, Olivetti and Graziano).

It is still possible to improve the quality of people's experience at work – and so to stimulate their initiative and enable them to take pride in what they do – even when technology is a constraint, as the sucessful case of General Motors' Tarrytown plant with its long assembly line demonstrates. Anything which demonstrates that people are not seen just as cogs in machines, but are valued for their ability to think critically about what they do, is potentially useful: for instance, increasing the control they have over decisions relating to their jobs and encouraging them to formulate and contribute ideas for improving productivity and quality, and so on. People tend not to be unreasonable about necessary constraints, as long as they understand and accept the reasons for them.

As well as changing technology and the nature of jobs, other complementary changes are likely to be necessary. For instance, we have seen how in the case studies the working environment has been improved, especially in factories, making it safer, healthier and more pleasant; Volvo describe it as the kind of environment that 'craftsmen' would be proud to enter. In most cases too the grading of jobs has been changed to take account of improvements in their professional content. Where appropriate, pay has been increased and pay systems adapted to make them more compatible with the new 'whole' jobs. Individual piece-work systems have given way to higher basic rates sometimes topped up by group bonuses.

While ancillary changes in pay and environment (or job 'context' as Herzberg would call it) are wholly appropriate, they should not be the main thrust of any programme of change. What nowadays distinguishes all major efforts to improve the way organizations work is the recognition that, important though it is to get them right, good pay and conditions do not stimulate the desire to do a good job. This stimulation comes only from having an interesting, challenging job and scope to take, or at least to influence, relevant decisions. This, therefore, is the type of job that organizations should aim to be creating.

Besides changing tangibles like jobs, working conditions, payment systems, technology and so on, the organization about to embark on changes will need to consider intangible matters: the 'perspective' of the organization (the extent to which it looks outwards towards its customers' needs, or inwards to servicing internal systems); the relationship between managers and subordinates; the kind of atmosphere and power structure that these relationships create; and the effect that these have on how people behave.

Put the customer first. Early attempts to improve the content of jobs, such as the job enrichment programmes of the 1960s, always took the customer's requirements into account because they aimed to improve productivity as well as job satisfaction. Nevertheless these early efforts did tend to look inwards at job content and company procedures rather than outwards to the customer. This emphasis was valuable at the time because it directed badly needed attention to the people doing the jobs and to the detrimental effects of not taking their needs sufficiently into account.

More recent efforts, however, tend to place more emphasis on the customer. The case of the British Civil Service, for instance, illustrates how the focus has shifted. In practice there is a subtle difference between asking 'how can these jobs be made more satisfying?' and 'how can these people be helped to do the best possible job?' The shift in emphasis does not mean that the people holding the jobs need to be exploited, far from it. As well as all the moral arguments against such exploitation it has not proved to be a secure basis for any operation in the past and will not do so today. There is a sense in which people find attempts to make their jobs more satisfying somewhat patronizing. However well intentioned, such attempts can so easily give the impression that the person holding the job is a 'dependent' for whom something is being be done.

When people are given the opportunity to decide for themselves how they should work, their first concern – once a few simple requirements have been met – is usually for their customers. They tend not to ask 'how would I like things to be?', but rather, 'what is sensible from the customer's point of view?' Thus, emphasizing the customer's requirements, as all the case studies do, is no bad thing for the employees. It increases the potential benefits of change by giving scope for people's natural instinct to do a good job. There need be no contradiction between operating in a business-like way and ensuring that employees enjoy a decent working experience. It is demoralizing for everyone concerned to work for an organization that is going downhill.

As well as the perspective of an organization there is also its 'atmosphere'. This may sound impossibly vague, but a change in the atmosphere of an organization which has begun to regenerate itself is often what strikes people most. One senior manager, when visiting projects to assess progress, described it in this way: 'the atmosphere in these offices feels different. In them I am met with lively, critical discussion and I get something out of it. In other offices I am met with polite agreement and I feel I have wasted my time.' In organizations where things feel like that people show more insight into the way their organization works, more initiative in deciding how improvements can be made and more enthusiasm in putting their ideas into practice. They are more critical of their organization, but at the same time more committed to it. There is a feeling of something thriving, rather than of people conscientiously plodding through their tasks.

This change in atmosphere is the vital ingredient of the new spirit of enterprise at which all the organizations examined here, including the British Civil Service, are aiming. The change arises from the fact that people have themselves been stimulated by the more stimulating jobs they are now doing, but just as important are the relationships between different levels of the organization. The manager of an office which had initiated a process of change put it as follows: 'we no longer divide ourselves into "managers" and "subordinates". We are just people with different responsibilities, doing different jobs to the best of our abilities.' And one of his 'subordinates' a year or so later said, 'before the project we used surnames in the office, especially if we were talking to the manager or one of the supervisors. Now we all use Christian names. But', she added, 'we are not in any doubt about who is the manager.'

How should we go about it?

Securing relationships that enable people to give of their best depends more than anything on the way in which an organization goes about deciding what should be done and then testing improvements. In fact the way that an organization goes about these things is the single most important factor in determining whether it thrives as an enterprise or not. The key to success is to be found in involving people at all levels in all aspects of the effort, from identifying what needs to be done, through designing and implementing improvements, through evaluation to applying what has been learnt.

This advice may provoke other questions. Isn't all this a needless and risky waste of time? Compared with experts like engineers, time study specialists and so on, don't those doing the job lack knowledge and experience, and compared with managers don't they lack vision? Won't they almost certainly take longer at first, and might they not make expensive mistakes? With these doubts in mind managers, trade union representatives and advisers alike may wish to take the apparent short cut of getting the experts and the managers to determine the changes and then 'selling' these ideas to the people who will be affected, even by flattering them into thinking that the ideas were actually their own. This path can be truly tempting. It looks as if it combines the best of both worlds: sensible, sophisticated changes efficiently arrived at, together with commitment aroused by the 'sales' effort.

However promising a change may look in theory, it will only work in practice if those doing the job are committed to making it work. All the evidence shows, that people are most likely to give their commitment to changes which they have themselves designed or influenced. Anybody else's change runs the risk of being seen as an imposed change and imposed change tends to arouse resentment rather than commitment.

Early projects set up in the British Civil Service, such as the one in the Inland Revenue, demonstrate how things tend to work in practice. In that case expert advisers suggested changes that made good theoretical sense but the projects were not so effective as later ones, like that in the DHSS, where people struggled through laboriously for themselves. Taking a very different illustration of the same point, Italsider judged it well worth while helping nine hundred of their employees to learn about new steelmaking processes in sufficient depth to enable them to contribute to the design of the new Genoa plant.

In practice there seem to be no short cuts. An organization needs the people who work for it to understand what they do, why they do it and how this relates to what others do. That sounds straightforward, but it is hard to accept and people have to learn from their own experience, not from that of others. They must be given time to have their own experience and find out things for themselves. This understanding is too important to be confined to managers and specialists. The more widespread it is, the firmer the footing of the organization and the greater its capacity for responding to its customers. Since it is this capacity that will keep it in business, it is worth spending the time necessary to develop it.

The importance of such involvement is now well established as common ground amongst advisers from many different backgrounds. The vital question is how to secure it without wasting valuable time. We must ask: 'in what should people be involved? And how should they be involved?' As the case studies show, there are a whole range of possibilities. What matters most is that the scope and method of involvement be right for the particular organization at the particular time.

Having said that, here are some basic ideas. As far as the scope of involvement is concerned, people should not be deliberately excluded from anything. Since all parts of an organization are linked no part should be allowed to be immune from change. This does not mean that all parts must change. It is simply that belief in the genuineness of the opportunity to change is undermined if people are asked, for example, to think about how the production process might be improved, but told to leave the sales department alone. This may conjure up visions of unproductive chaos in which no decisions can ever be taken because unmanageable numbers of untrained, incapable people get in the way. But in practice this is not a difficulty. People do not usually want to be involved beyond the extent of their competence. Management's main problem is how to encourage people to use the abilities they have rather than to persuade them to keep out of areas in which they are not competent.

In the early days especially, there may be disagreements between managers and their subordinates about where involvement is appropriate. For instance, in one social security office the manager was convinced that junior staff and their supervisors were going beyond their competence in attempting to reorganize their section. For their part the staff saw the manager as both unwilling to relax his hold and ignorant of the problems that they wanted to solve. The manager sensed that this was a vital issue. If he 'interfered' he would confirm the junior staff's impression that he did not trust them. Also in preventing them from making mistakes he would be preventing them from learning. On the other hand, if he allowed the junior staff to try out their plan, time might be wasted and the public might be inconvenienced.

The manager wrote afterwards:

the situation did develop almost to crisis point and just when I had reached the stage of serious alarm the . . . supervisors asked me to attend a meeting to help in the resolution of the position. It was a very good meeting. I was impressed by the serious and constructive approach which the supervisors made and with the high level of their discussion. I was content to fall quite naturally into my new role. I no longer wished to 'push' solutions. I offered advice as it was asked and took no more than an equal share in the discussion. . . . The meeting was a break-through as far as I was concerned. . . . I felt a sudden sense of relief, as I suddenly became aware that, of course, I could trust them. They knew every bit as much about the details of the projected task as myself and they were indeed a concientious and hard-working group. I have felt more relaxed ever since.

The meeting was a breakthrough for the junior staff and supervisors too. The fact that the manager had held back despite his anxieties convinced them that he was indeed sincere in offering them more influence (a fact that they had doubted before). They also saw that he understood more about their problems than they had previously suspected and that his wider experience could be of service to them.

This may seem like a time-consuming way to learn a simple lesson. But managers and their subordinates who have taken part in projects in all sorts of organizations tell similar stories. The limits of involvement cannot be set in advance. They can only be established through experience and they will keep changing as experience grows. A good starting point is to involve people right from the beginning in determining what the project should be about or what the organization's problem are – not in a vague, generalized sense, but in concrete everyday operational terms. What, for instance, do people find gets in the way of their doing a good job? What procedures help · them; what procedures waste their time? Where might they save time? How might they put it to better use? What do they feel they should be doing that they are not doing at present? What additional training and support do they need? What aspects of their jobs do they find satisfying?

Encouraging people to identify the problems they want to work on and the strong points that they would like to build on is the first step in gaining their commitment to the change process. The problem must be 'owned' by them, not by someone else. Encouraging people to analyse and come to grips with their problem is the surest way of building up a widespread understanding of how the organization really works. It is also the best way for an organization to tap the fund of its employees' experience. This is why the DHSS felt it worth-while for its project team to spend nine months working with the staff of its local office in Swansea and interviewing all two hundred of them individually. From a different standpoint and for quite different motives, it is why the Italian trade unions want their members to be involved in projects designed to change organizations.

The next stage is to involve people in analysing problems in this way and still go on doing a day's work. A whole battery of techniques is available. But again the answer is that it matters far less what method is chosen than that it has some basis in common sense and that people do not feel that it has been imposed on them. I have seen identical methods for analysing problems succeed brilliantly and fail abysmally. I have seen crude, unsophisticated questionnaires provide information which has been acted upon successfully and seen well-conceived, professional questionnaires provide information which was simply shelved. The crucial point seems to be whether the method, or questionnaire, belonged to 'the experts' or to the people concerned.

This process of trying to understand the problems which need to be solved is not a once and for all matter. Problems change and so do people's understanding of them. So, once the enquiry process is established it should be developed, not just for any predetermined 'project phase', but as part of the normal way of working. Individual interviews, group discussions, questionnaires, various means of analysing job content and the extent of authority may all play their part in getting the process going. Working parties and other committees might be established to facilitate the formal asking of questions such as how well does the organization meet the needs of its customers; what do people think of working in this organization; what do they think of the jobs they do; and how can the organization make better use of its people?

Saab found their 'production' and 'development' groups useful both in promoting and continuing this process. Some General Motors plants found that meetings of workers and supervisors along the lines of 'quality circles' were helpful. Volvo and parts of the British Civil Service held similar meetings, but without labelling them in this way. Such formality must gradually fade away. Ultimately what matters is whether people use their experience and initiative from day to day; whether there is co-operation between colleagues; and trust and good two-way communication between colleagues and between people and their immediate boss.

Once this process of involvement is under way it will need constant encouragement and reinforcement. A powerful way of providing such encouragement – and an essential means of reinforcing the process of enquiry – is to ensure that people do more than identify problems and put forward suggested solutions. They must also be offered the opportunity to turn their ideas into testable propositions and to try them out in practice. This in turn means that people will have to put in more thought and make greater use of their experience and initiative. They will then learn far more about the way their organization works and so will become better equipped to help change it. They will become more committed to making changes work than they would if someone else took their ideas and translated them into practical propositions for them. In addition, those taking part will gain far more satisfaction from their efforts and their organization will gain a more skilled and insightful workforce. If the organization is not prepared to go this far it will deprive itself of some of these potential benefits, as well as depriving its employees of some of their satisfaction. This was what went wrong at the DHSS, Swansea, when the advisers proposed a new organization structure based on people's ideas, rather than encouraging them to go through the whole process for themselves.

To consolidate this process of involvement people at all levels should also take part in evaluating what is being achieved – and this is dealt with in more detail below under the question: 'how do we know if we are on the right track?'

So much for the people inside the organization. The customers outside also have an interest in changes in organization and they too have a potential contribution to make. The case studies show that the first steps in this direction have been taken. Volvo, for instance, does from time to time consult some of its distributors. Swedish and Italian companies tend to discuss proposed new development with local communities. Some of the projects in the British Civil Service have forged stronger customer links. However so far this is all rudimentary. In my view there is a huge untapped potential. A greater involvement of the customer in changing organizations – particularly, but not exclusively, in the service sector – could benefit employees by making their customers more real to them and could benefit customers by helping them to get what they want from the organization and from the people in it. In this way the organization must surely benefit too.

Projects which aim at bringing about radical change need a framework and every organization will establish its own, depending on custom and legal requirements. In Sweden, for instance, laws require companies to work with employee representatives, and the practices of companies like Volvo have long been in advance of such laws. In France and Italy works councils exist with the express purpose of providing a framework for employee involvement, but in a different way and against a different cultural background than in Sweden and Germany. In France and Italy the situation is not so advanced as in Scandinavia and Germany, and many French and Italian works councils are little more than ciphers.

Although there is no legally established 'Industrial Democracy' in the UK, organizations nevertheless work within an accepted industrial relations framework. In the Civil Service all project activity has taken place within the framework of the Whitley system of joint consultation, using existing joint committees wherever possible and establishing new ones where necessary. British Leyland also used their normal industrial relations machinery as the framework, supplemented, until its suspension, by its employee participation scheme.

Whatever the existing framework for involvement, it is sensible to start with it. From the beginning there is the vital task of ensuring that the aims and progress of the project are clearly and quickly communicated throughout the organization. Rumours endanger everything. Although eventually everyone will have the responsibility for this communication, it makes sense to use existing channels in the early days. The project work may itself demonstrate how existing frameworks can be modified, as it did in the Civil Service, resulting in new local joint consultation bodies as well as a new National Joint Steering Group. If machinery of this kind is ignored problems always result. Managers, trade unions and employee representatives can come to feel that their authority is being undermined and so turn against the whole effort.

However sophisticated it is, such machinery alone can never give life to democracy. That can only be built up from involvement in simple, but important, day-to-day matters towards involvement in more complex issues.

Such long-term processes of change of the kind described which potentially involve all the people and functions in an organization and even the customer, need the clear support of both senior managers and trade union representatives, ideally backed up by the appointment of some kind of core group to co-ordinate the whole process. This is an obvious point, but it is not as straightforward as it may appear. It is not just a matter of top managers and trade union representatives stating their support, however unequivocally. They must demonstrate it and go on doing so. They must show by their own behaviour that they, too, are willing to reconsider and to change, like the manager quoted above, who held back his advice until it was asked for and then gave it wholeheartedly.

It is often hard for senior people to accept that their subordinates – or, in the case of trade union representatives, their members – do not accept that those above them are totally committed to change. It is even harder for them to come to terms with the fact that such doubts are often realistic in view of past behaviour. It is usually only through the experience of a project that senior managers and trade union representatives can learn about the effects of their normal way of operating and so adjust their behaviour. In fact, despite all the sincere statements of intent issued at the beginning of such projects, genuine top level commitment is something which can only develop as understanding grows. It is communicated more by actions than by words and shows as much in what people do not do as in what they do. People cannot really be committed until they understand what the commitment entails. It is quite common, therefore, for much of a programme of change to run with only patchy top level support and understanding.

While the full potential of such programmes will not be realized without full support, projects of the kind described often prove themselves to be remarkably tenacious and resilient. Once they have made a start people who really believe in the projects will make quite superhuman efforts to keep them alive. There is, in this sense, a way in which nothing can ever be quite the same again once one of these projects has started. As one participant said, 'You cannot unhave an experience you have had.'

The tenacity of such projects frightens senior people – not unnaturally, because they sense that once those at junior level have experienced their new-found freedom they will be unwilling to give it up. Senior people sometimes therefore fear that they are being asked to commit themselves to a process which may have irreversible consequences. They are afraid that this means abdicating their responsibilities, and that in agreeing that people should be free to try out new ways of working they are committing themselves to accepting the new ways no matter what the consequences turn out to be. This need not be so.

What is needed for experimentation to flourish is not unquestioning acceptance, by those at the top, of the consequences of change but, rather, a willingness that experimentation should take place, and that people should find things out for themselves. It would indeed be irresponsible for senior managers to stand by while the organization and its customers suffered, just as it would be irresponsible for senior trade union representatives to stand by while the legitimate interests of their members were threatened. There must be a balance. People must feel that the opportunity to use their initiative is genuine, otherwise their imagination will not be stimulated. But they do value advice when it is given in the right spirit and at the right time. What they do not respect is a senior who stands aloof, indicating silent disapproval instead of helping.

How do we know if we are on the right track?

I see evaluation as one of the most critical aspects of the whole process. It is critical for two reasons: first, if the change process is to be valuable it must mean that people are stepping into the unknown and taking risks. They will be trying out new ways of working and new ways of relating to each other. They will be taking on new kinds of responsibilities and trying to acquire new kinds of skills. The management will quite naturally want to know how well this is turning out; whether productivity, quality and service to the customer is benefiting or suffering as a result. People lower down the organization will also want to assess progress since they too have a sense of responsibility which needs to be satisfied.

Secondly one of the distinguishing features of a responsive organization is that its employees are able to learn all the time from what they are doing and to apply what they are learning. Evaluation of a process which aims to create this responsiveness serves to help clarify what is being learnt and ensure that it is being applied. This was the purpose behind the evaluation conferences held in the Northern and Yorks and Humberside regions of the DHSS.

Given these two purposes of evaluation, what sort of evaluation might be helpful? First, people throughout the organization must be encouraged to take part – and this includes trade union representatives who, in addition, may wish to carry out their own evaluation. Involving people in determining and implementing change stimulates their imagination, releases their initiative and secures their commitment. Involving them in evaluating what they have done gives them responsibility and enables them to learn from what they have done and to apply what they have learnt. This may seem self-evident, but for some managers it can seem too risky. Having taken the risk of letting people decide what to do, managers are comforted by the thought that they can themselves decide whether what has happened is a good thing which should be continued, or a bad thing which should be stopped. Unless they reinforce the first stage by encouraging people at the second stage to evaluate for themselves, they will be seen to be behaving in an inconsistent, contradictory way, and this inconsistency will cast doubt on the genuineness of their willingness to share responsibility. Of course managers, like everyone else concerned, should play their part in evaluating the process in particular by contributing perspective. They have a responsibility to the organization, but if they do not share this responsibility the whole process will be undermined.

Secondly, the case studies show that, important though statistics of productivity and quality are, there is more to evaluation than output figures. Attitudes and opinions are also valuable, and all the organizations in the case studies had collected details of these, by questionnaires, interviews and both formal and informal discussions. Questionnaires and interviews are important, but genuine discussion is invaluable because it means a two-way exchange and this is what most facilitates learning. Real evaluation means discussion of how intangible matters like relationships and atmosphere have changed and what the consequences of any such changes have been. Such discussion means reconciling different, sometimes contradictory, views about crucial issues like sharing power and control between managers and those at more junior levels.

Were the managers at Fiat wise to abandon the 'island' assembly experiment at their Rivalta plant? Were the operational difficulties really so great, or was it, as the trade unions contend, that management 'could not cope ideologically' with giving those who did the job sufficient scope to solve the problems? In essence, this is what evaluating change is about. There is much to be gained and lost in the process of evaluation because people invest their emotions in it. More than anything else it is the genuineness and openness of evaluation that determines how much can be learned and put to good use in improving the experience of employee and customer.

And what about the customer? The logical extension of the process of involving all those affected within the organization is, surely, to involve those affected outside. Here we still have a long way to go; but what about asking some customers for their views on relevant questions? After all, where they are directly affected by what you are attempting, only the customers can give you the information you need to assess whether or not you are on the right track.

What sort of help might we need and where can we get it?

The anxiety caused by such a process of change is a normal and inevitable human reaction to taking a step into the unknown, to re-evaluating habitual behaviour and to learning to behave differently especially if it is combined with meeting normal job responsibilities. Such anxiety is not confined to any particular age or grade. It occurs in young and old alike, in senior and junior grades in the office and on the shop floor and amongst trade union representatives as well as managers. Some people are by temperament more inclined to accept such challenges than others, and their enthusiasm is useful in getting the process going, but enthusiasm can bring its own problems. It can tempt people to move ahead without proper, but time-consuming, consideration of options and consultation with interested parties. It can mask a desire to right real or imagined wrongs of the past. It can threaten those who are naturally inclined to move more slowly.

People need help if they are to find their way through, making constructive use of enthusiasm and paying sympathetic attention to genuine fears, irrational as well as rational. In their different ways all the organizations we have examined here found it necessary to offer this kind of help. All of them provided training in special skills like supportive management and effective group-working. Some, in addition, used advisers to provide more specialized help. Such advisers might come both from within the organization and from outside; both have a particular role to play. They should all be skilled in helping people through a process of change. Those from within can provide inside knowledge of how their organization works and of some of the key personalities involved. However, because they are themselves part of the structure, the progress of their own career is inevitably affected by how they work as advisers. This can limit their impact at crucial times. For instance, it takes a brave, some would say foolhardy, person to press an authoritarian personnel director to examine the way he treats his subordinates, when it is the personnel director who decides whether or not the adviser is promoted.

In supporting and advising senior managers, an outsider can be vital. The external consultant is not governed by considerations like promotion within the organization, although he or she faces other pressures – the need to earn fees, for instance. But there are times when the view of the outsider with his experience of going through similar processes in other organizations is very helpful indeed. The outsider can also be an asset in helping trade union representatives work through their own problems – a situation in which internal advisers can find their effectiveness reduced because their independence is, rightly or wrongly, suspect.

What do advisers do day by day? They do certain obvious things: explain the aims of the project clearly and ensure that they are understood; hold interviews; devise, issue and analyse questionnaires; run training sessions, report on progress; and ensure that this is communicated efficiently throughout the organization; assist in evaluation; and advise on longer-term strategy. But, as with so many aspects of this type of change, it is the less visible side of things which is so important. The effectiveness of advisers in helping people to change constructively lies more than anything else in the kind of personal relationships that they establish with key individuals at all levels in the organization, and amongst trade union representatives. It is a matter of how far the advisers are trusted. Are they seen as being independent? Do they appear to understand the realities of life in the organization and the problems, personal as well as organizational of changing it? The better advisers can communicate with all kinds of people the more effective they are likely to be, for they will have to find out how people feel about their jobs, about procedures and about relationships within the organization. They will have to help people to understand their own feelings and the feelings that their behaviour arouses in others and, more difficult than helping people understand, they will have to encourage them to find the confidence to act on this understanding.

Advisers can be under many conflicting pressures. They must always be ready to listen sympathetically, but listening alone is not enough. They must help people to act too. This can mean bringing people face to face with feelings and issues that they would prefer to avoid, helping them to find the courage to take risks that they would prefer not to take. Advisers must always beware of allowing people to become dependent, and of being persuaded to take the decisions and actions that people are afraid to take themselves. If they fall into this trap they run the risk of being the scapegoat if things go wrong and, worse, they encourage dependence rather than the independence which is essential if confident innovation is to get under way.

It is not always easy for advisers to resist such pressures. Theirs is often a lonely job and like any human being they probably like to be liked. It can be tempting to tackle difficult issues for people – to have a quiet word in the pub with the manager on behalf of his subordinates rather than encourage those subordinates to face up to talking to him themselves; or to pass on the news about a new development rather than to ensure that people take the responsibility of keeping their colleagues properly informed. If advisers do things for people they are not doing their job; their job is to help people to do things for themselves.

If the change process is genuine, mistakes are inevitable and so are doubts and disagreements. There is no avoiding them, nor should there be because, gruelling though the experience may be at the time, they often prove to be the substance of the whole process. It is through mistakes more than anything else that people learn – always providing, of course, that they are constructively used. Here again advisers can play a crucial part, in helping people to see exactly what the problem is and where the disagreement lies and why. Without their support there is always the danger that people will give up too easily, allowing their doubts and disagreements to overwhelm them rather than to help create the new understanding that they are seeking.

Because the adviser's effectiveness depends so much on personal relationships, it is important that an organization uses only advisers that are 'right' for it. Knowledge and a good track record of appropriate experience are important of course, but they must not be packaged up in some standard technique, nor are they by themselves enough. The advisers and key people in the organization must be comfortable with each other because they will have to go through a lot together and they will all be affected by what they achieve, or fail to achieve, together.

Summary

So, to sum up, what would I say if I were asked by a client for a list of the main points to be borne in mind by an organization seeking to thrive in the difficult circumstances of today?

1. Accept that the process of change must be continuous.
2. Avoid packaged techniques for change. There is no substitute for working things through yourself, learning from experience as you go.
3. Look outwards to your customers, involving them as much as possible in determining your problems and in assessing the effectiveness of your improvements.
4. Involve all people and all functions in your organization – including the trade unions when you have them – in the whole process from the determination of problems and options, through putting ideas into practice, to evaluating their effects and applying what has been learnt.
5. Accept that no level or function of the organization should be beyond the scope of change.
6. Start from where you are. Use existing channels and structures and modify them as experience with a project suggests is necessary.
7. Beware of rumours. Ensure that communication is quick and clear and that it reaches all that it should reach and that they have understood the message.

8. Make sure that top managers and trade union representatives are willing to support freedom to experiment and make sure that their willingness is clearly communicated. If necessary appoint people to co-ordinate and clarify the process.

9. Don't be put off by mistakes and disagreements. Use them constructively.

10. If possible get independent outside advice. Don't go for an adviser who is peddling a standard package. Go for one with experience of helping people to do things for themselves and with whom you feel you can work compatibly.

Notes

Chapter 2. Working in organizations – why things go wrong

1. Abraham H. Maslow, *Motivation and Personality* (2nd edn., New York, 1970).
2. Douglas McGregor, *The Human Side of Enterprise* (New York, 1960).
3. William Ouchi, *Theory Z: How American Business Can Meet Japanese Challenge* (Reading, Massachusetts, 1981).
4. Frederick Herzberg, B. Mausner, B. Snyderman, *The Motivation to Work* (2nd edn., New York, 1967).

Chapter 3. Working in organizations – attempts at improvement

1. Frederick Winslow Taylor, *The Principles of Scientific Management* (New York, 1911).
2. R. F. Hoxie, *Scientific Management and Labor* (New York, 1915). Useful extracts from this report are given in Lisl Klein, *New Forms of Work Organisation* (Cambridge, 1976).
3. F. J. Roethlisberger and W. J. Dickson, *Management and the Worker* (Cambridge, Massachusetts, 1939).
4. W. W. Daniel and Neil McIntosh, *The Right to Manage* (London, 1972). This PEP report gives a brief summary of the work these companies carried out – covering reasons for action, changes made and results achieved, plus suggestions for further reading.
5. For brief descriptions of various applications and details of further reading see Lisl Klein, *New Forms of Work Organization*.

Introduction to the case studies

1. Useful accounts of comparisons between Japanese and Western styles of operating can be found in William Ouchi, *Theory Z* and in R. Dore, *British Factory – Japanese Factory* (London, 1973).

Chapter 4. The motor manufacturing industry

1. For an authoritative and highly readable account of Volvo's philosophy and of some of the key changes they introduced see Pehr G. Gyllenhammar, *People at Work* (Reading, Massachusetts, 1977).
2. A report made for the European Foundation for the Improvement of Living and Working Conditions, *The Impact of New Technology on*

Shiftwork in the Automobile Industry, by Christine Howarth in December 1982. This report also summarizes details of the most significant forms of new technology in use in car manufacturing.

3. Christine Howarth, *Impact of New Technology* .
4. Stefan Agurén, Reine Hansson, K. G. Carlsson , *The Volvo Kalmar Plant – The Impact of New Design on Work Organisation* (Stockholm, 1976).
5. Jan-Peder Norstedt and Stefan Agurén, *The Saab-Scania Report* (Stockholm, 1973). This booklet gives a useful summary of the early work at Saab-Scania, culminating in the design and commissioning of the new petrol engine plant.

Further reading

A. Background and Theory

C. Argyris, *Integrating the Individual and the Organization* (Wiley, New York, 1964)

W. G. Bennis, *Changing Organizations* (McGraw-Hill, New York, 1966)

Huw Beynon, *Working for Ford* (Allen Lane, Harmondsworth, 1973)

R. Blauner, *Alienation and Freedom* (University of Chicago Press, 1964)

T. Burns and G. M. Stalker, *The Management of Innovation* (2nd edn., Tavistock, London, 1966)

L. E. Davis and J. C. Taylor, *Design of Jobs* (Penguin, Harmondsworth, 1972)

Peter F. Drucker, *The Age of Discontinuity* (Heinemann, London, 1971)

F. E. Emery and E. Thorsrud, *Form and Content in Industrial Democracy* (Tavistock, London, 1969)

John C. Glidewell, *Choice Points* (MIT Press, Cambridge, Mass., 1970)

A. W. Gouldner, *Patterns of Industrial Bureaucracy* (Routledge, London, 1955)

P. G. Herbst, *Socio-Technical Design* (Tavistock, London, 1974)

F. Herzberg, B. Mausner, B. Snyderman, *The Motivation to Work* (2nd edn., John Wiley and Sons, New York, 1967)

D. Katz and R. L. Kahn, *The Social Psychology of Organizations* (John Wiley & Sons, New York, 1966)

R. Likert, *New Patterns of Management* (McGraw-Hill, New York, 1961)

A. H. Maslow, *Motivation and Personality* (2nd edn., Harper and Row, New York, 1970)

Douglas McGregor, *The Human Side of Enterprise* (McGraw-Hill, New York, 1960)

Douglas McGregor, *The Professional Manager* (McGraw-Hill, New York, 1967)

William Ouchi, *Theory Z: How American Business Can Meet Japanese Challenge* (Addison-Wesley, Reading, Mass., 1981)

E. H. Schein, *Organizational Psychology* (Prentice-Hall, Englewood Cliffs, N.J., 1965)

F. W. Taylor, *The Principles of Scientific Management* (Harper and Row, New York, 1911)

J. M. Thomas and W. G. Bennis, *Management of Change and Conflict* (Penguin Books, Harmondsworth, 1972)

Alvin Toffler, *Future Shock* (Pan Books, London, 1973)

Karl E. Weick, *The Social Psychology of Organizing* (Addison-Wesley Publishing Co.Inc., Reading, Mass., 1969)

Colin Wilson, *New Pathways in Psychology: Maslow and the Post-Freudian Revolution* (Victor Gollancz, London, 1972)

Gerald Zaltman, Philip Kotler and Ira Kaufman (edd.), *Creating Social Change* (Holt, Rinehart and Winston, New York, 1972)

B. Improving the quality of working life in practice

S. Agurén, R. Hansson and K. G. Karlsson, *The Volvo Kalmar Plant: The Impact of New Design on Work Organization* (Rationalization Council SAF-LO, Stockholm, 1976)

A. F. Alber, 'How (and how not) to approach job enrichment', *Personnel Journal*, Vol: 58, No. 12 (December 1979), pp. 837-41, 867

A. Alioth et al. (edd.), *Working on the Quality of Working Life* (Martinus Nijhoff, Leiden, 1978)

ANACT, 'Organization of work and working conditions in Italy – report of a meeting of French and Italian trade unionists and researchers (Organisation et conditions de travail en Italie: compte rendu d'une rencontre Franco-Italienne de syndicalistes et chercheurs)', Paris: ANACT, Lille, University of Lille, 1978

A. Barry, 'Why Cummins engines Daventry connection paid off handsomely', *Engineer*, Vol. 246, No. 6365 (23 March 1978), pp. 26-7

D. Birchall, C. Carnall and R. Wild, 'The development of group working in biscuit manufacture – a case', *Personnel Review*, Vol. 7, No. 2 (Spring 1978), pp. 40-9

I. Bluestone, 'Creating a new world of work', *International Labour Review*, Vol. 115, No. 1 (Jan–Feb. 1977), pp. 1-10

S. Cameron, *Job Satisfaction: The Concept and its Measurement* (Work Research Unit, London, 1973, WRU occasional paper No. 4)

S. Cameron, *Organisational Change: a Description of Alternative Strategies* (Work Research Unit, London, 1973, WRU Occasional Paper No. 5)

Dr C. A. Carnall, *The Evaluation of Organisational Change* (Gower Press, London, 1982)

C. L. Cooper and E. Mumford, *The Quality of Working Life in Western and Eastern Europe* (Associated Business Press, London, 1979)

L. E. Davis and A. B. Cherns, *The Quality of Working Life: vol. 1, Problems, Prospects and the State of the Art* (The Free Press, New York, 1975)

L. E. Davis and A. B. Cherns, *The Quality of Working Life: vol. 2, Cases and Commentary* (The Free Press, New York, 1975)

F. J. den Hertog, 'The search for new leads in job design: the Philips case', *Journal of Contemporary Business*, vol. 6, No. 3 (Spring 1977), pp. 49-66

R.N. Ford, 'Job Enrichment Lessons from AT and T', *Harvard Business Review* (Jan–Feb 1973), pp. 96-106

P.G. Gyllenhammar, *People at Work* (Addison-Wesley, Reading, Mass., 1977)

P. Hill, *Towards a New Philosophy of Management – A Study of the Company Development Programme at Shell-UK Ltd.* (Gower Press, London, 1971)

D. Hull, *The Shop Stewards' Guide to Work Organization* (Spokesman Books, Nottingham, 1979)

International Institute for Labour Studies, *Implications for Trade Unions of the Trend Towards New Forms of Work Organization* (IILS, Geneva, 1977)

L. Klein, *New Forms of Work Organisation* (Cambridge University Press, Cambridge, 1976)

L. Klein, *A Social Scientist in Industry* (Gower Press, London, 1976)

E. Mumford and D. Henshall, *A Participative Approach to Computer Systems Design: a Case Study of the Introduction of a New Computer System* (Associated Business Press, London, 1979)

J.-P. Norstedt and S. Agurén, *The Saab-Scania Report* (SAF, Stockholm, 1973)

F. Novara, 'Job Enrichment in the Olivetti Company', *International Labour Review*, vol. 108, No. 4 (Oct, 1973), pp. 283-94

S. Russell, *Quality Circles in Perspective* (Work Research Unit, London, 1983, WRU Occasional Paper No. 24)

R. G. Sell, *Microelectronics and the Quality of Working Life* (Work Research Unit, D. E., London, 1980, WRU Occasional Paper No. 17)

M. Weir and S. Mills, 'The supervisor as a change catalyst', *Industrial Relations Journal*, vol. 4, No. 4 (Winter 1973), pp. 61-9

W. A. Westley, 'The role of the supervisor in quality of working life programs', *Quality of Working Life – The Canadian Scene*, vol. 3, No. 2 (1980), pp. 2-7

The Work Research Unit at the Department of Employment will supply, free of charge, useful bibliographies on a wide range of subjects related to the theory and practice of improving the quality of working life. Contact:

The Librarian,
The Work Research Unit,
Steel House,
Tothill Street,
London SW1H 9NF.

Tel. 01-213 4702.

Index

OPUS General Editors

Keith Thomas
Alan Ryan
Peter Medawar

OPUS books provide concise, original, and authoritative introductions to a wide range of subjects in the humanities and sciences. They are written by experts for the general reader as well as for students.

Most of the titles listed here are only available in paperback editions; some are available in both hardback and paperback, and a few in hardback only. For further details contact the General Publicity Department, Oxford University Press, Walton Street, Oxford OX2 6DP.

Architecture

The Shapes of Structure
Heather Martienssen

Economics

The Economics of Money
A. C. L. Day

History

The Industrial Revolution
1760–1830
T. S. Ashton

Karl Marx
His Life and Environment
Isaiah Berlin

Early Modern France,
1560–1715
Robin Briggs

Modern Spain, 1875–1980
Raymond Carr

The Workshop of the World
British Economic History from
1820–1880
J. D. Chambers

English Towns in Transition,
1500–1700
Peter Clark and Paul Slack

The Economy of England,
1450–1750
Donald C. Coleman

The Impact of English Towns,
1700–1800
P. J. Corfield

The Russian Revolution,
1917–1932
Sheila Fitzpatrick

War in European History
Michael Howard

England and Ireland since 1800
Patrick O'Farrell

Louis XIV
David Ogg

The First World War
Keith Robbins

The French Revolution
J. M. Roberts

The Voice of the Past
Oral History
Paul Thompson

Town, City, and Nation
England 1850–1914
P. J. Waller

Britain in the Age of Economic
Management
An Economic History since 1939
John Wright

Law

Law and Modern Society
P. S. Atiyah
forthcoming

Introduction to English Law
Revised Edition
William Geldart

English Courts of Law
*H. G. Hanbury and
D. C. M. Yardley*

Literature

The Modern American Novel
Malcolm Bradbury

This Stage-Play World
English Literature and its
Background, 1580–1625
Julia Briggs

Medieval Writers and their Work
English Literature and its
Background, 1100–1500
J. A. Burrow

Romantics, Rebels and
Reactionaries
English Literature and its
Background, 1760–1830
Marilyn Butler

Ancient Greek Literature
Kenneth Dover and others

British Theatre since 1955
Ronald Hayman

Modern English Literature
W. W. Robson

Mathematics

What is Mathematical Logic?
J. N. Crossley and others

Medical Sciences

What is Psychotherapy?
Sidney Bloch

Man Against Disease
Preventive Medicine
J. A. Muir Gray

Philosophy

Aristotle the Philosopher
J. L. Ackrill

The Standing of Psychoanalysis
B. A. Farrell

The Character of Mind
Colin McGinn

Moral Philosophy
D. D. Raphael

The Problems of Philosophy
Bertrand Russell

Structuralism and Since
From Lévi-Strauss to Derrida
Edited by John Sturrock

Free Will and Responsibility
Jennifer Trusted

Ethics since 1900
Mary Warnock

Existentialism
Mary Warnock

Politics and International Affairs

Devolution
Vernon Bogdanor

Marx's Social Theory
Terrell Carver

Contemporary International Theory and the Behaviour of States
Joseph Frankel

International Relations in a Changing World
Joseph Frankel

The Life and Times of Liberal Democracy
C. B. Macpherson

The Nature of American Politics
H. G. Nicholas

English Local Government Reformed
Lord Redcliffe-Maud and Bruce Wood

Religion

An Introduction to the Philosophy of Religion
Brian Davies

Islam
An Historical Survey
H. A. R. Gibb

What is Theology?
Maurice Wiles

Hinduism
R. C. Zaehner

Science

The Philosophies of Science
An Introductory Survey
R. Harré

A Historical Introduction to the Philosophy of Science
J. P. Losee

The Structure of the Universe
Jayant V. Narlikar

Violent Phenomena in the Universe
Jayant V. Narlikar

What is Ecology?
Denis F. Owen

Energy: A Guidebook
Janet Ramage

Social Sciences

Change in British Society
A. H. Halsey

Towns and Cities
Emrys Jones

Social Anthropology
Godfrey Lienhardt

Races of Africa
C. G. Seligman

Urban Planning in Rich and Poor
Countries
Hugh Stretton